Risk Management in Organizations

In any organization, risk plays a huge role in the success or failure of any business endeavour. Measuring and managing risk is a difficult and often complicated task, and the global financial crisis of the late noughties can be traced to a worldwide deficiency in risk management regimes. One of the problems in understanding how best to manage risk is a lack of detailed examples of real world practice.

In this accessible textbook the author sets the world of risk management in the context of the broader corporate governance agenda, as well as explaining the core elements of a risk management system. Material on the differences between risk management and internal auditing is supplemented by a section on the professionalization of risk – a relatively contemporary evolution. Enterprise risk management is also fully covered.

With a detailed array of risk management cases – including Tesco, RBS and the UK government – lecturers will find this a uniquely well researched resource, supplemented by materials that enable the cases to be easily integrated into the classroom. Risk managers will be delighted with the case materials made available for the first time with the publication of this book.

Margaret Woods is Reader in Accounting at Aston Business School, Aston University, UK, and the co-ordinator of the European Risk Research Forum. She has published numerous articles in both academic and practitioner journals, and her research on bank risk and related issues has stimulated local and national media interest.

Risk Management in Organizations

An integrated case study approach

Margaret Woods

Routledge
Taylor & Francis Group

LONDON AND NEW YORK

First published 2011
by Routledge
2 Park Square, Milton Park, Abingdon, Oxon. OX14 4RN

Simultaneously published in the USA and Canada
by Routledge
711 Third Ave, New York, NY 10017

Routledge is an imprint of the Taylor & Francis Group, an informa business

British Library Cataloguing in Publication Data
A catalogue record for this book is available from the British Library

Library of Congress Cataloging in Publication Data
Woods, Margaret, 1954–
Risk management in organizations: an integrated case study approach
Margaret Woods. – 1st ed.
    p. cm.
Includes bibliographical references and index.
1. Risk management. 2. Management–Research. I. Title.
HD61.W66 2011
658.15'5–dc22

2010048412

ISBN: 978-0-415-59172-0 (hbk)
ISBN: 978-0-415-59173-7 (pbk)
ISBN: 978-0-203-81592-2 (ebk)

The Author and Publisher gratefully acknowledge the permission granted
to reproduce the copyright material in this book and report the research
results for each case study. Every effort has been made to trace copyright
holders and interviewees to obtain their permission for the use of the
material. The Publisher apologizes for any errors or omissions and would
be grateful if notified of any corrections that should be incorporated in
future reprints or editions of this book.

Typeset in Times New Roman
by Glyph International

Contents

List of illustrations	viii
List of tables	ix
List of boxes	x
Acknowledgements	xi
Foreword (CIMA)	xii
Foreword (IRM)	xiv

Introduction — 1

1 How to use this book — 4

Guidance notes for academic use 4
Guidance notes for practitioner use 5

PART I
Governance and risk management — 7

2 Risk and governance — 9

Aim 9
Risk management and corporate governance 9
Two phases of regulatory change 10
'Hard' versus 'soft' laws of governance 18
Conclusion 19

3 Risk and control — 22

Aim 22
Risk categories 22
Standards for risk management and enterprise risk management 27
Who is responsible for risk management? 39
Conclusion 42

PART II
Risk management in practice (1) The private sector   45

4   Case study: Tesco PLC   47

Company profile 47
Sources of data reported in the case study 50
Risk management: an overview 50
Risk management within Tesco: internal influences 51
Governance 55
Linking risk management to performance management 60
The risk management framework 66
Risk reporting and communication 68
The big challenge: extending the risk management
  system into Tesco Personal Finance 68
Conclusion 70

5   Case study: Royal Bank of Scotland   72

Company profile 72
Sources of data reported in the case study 74
Key observations 75
Introduction 75
External influences on risk management in banks 76
Overview of the risk management approach
  in the Royal Bank of Scotland 81
Risk ownership, operating oversight and reporting lines 90
Conclusion: the group-wide impact of the risk
  management structure 93

PART III
Risk management in practice (2) The public sector   97

6   Case study: the Department of Culture, Media and Sport   99

Government exposure to risk 99
Historical background 99
Generic versus domain-specific approaches to
  public sector risk management 103
Profile of the Department of Culture, Media and Sport 106
Risk framework within the DCMS 109
Internal audit 121

Self-assessment 122
The big challenge: the management of partnership risk 124
Update 125

7 Case study: Birmingham City Council 127

Risk and governance 127
Historical background 128
Autonomy in the design of risk management systems 129
Sources of data reported in the case study 130
Corporate profile 130
Risk management in Birmingham City Council 133
The risk management framework 137
The big challenge: linking risk to performance management 146
Conclusion 152

PART IV
Key lessons for the future 153

8 Lessons from the case studies 155

Aim 155
Overview of the case studies 155
Risk management in context 156
The big challenge: implementing a three-dimensional system 159
Summary 163
Lessons from the public sector 164
Conclusion 166

Notes 168
Index 170

List of illustrations

3.1	Risk rankings by category	23
3.2	The COSO cube	30
3.3	Linking the three components of ISO 31000	31
3.4	Risk register template	35
3.5	Likelihood: consequences matrix	36
3.6	Risk architecture of a large PLC	38
4.1	Governance model	56
4.2	'Our steering wheel'	57
4.3	Cause and effect in the steering wheel	58
4.4	Linking strategy to performance to risk management	61
4.5	Core elements of the risk management process	67
4.6	Communication lines in Tesco	69
5.1	The FSA's portfolio of firms as at August 2006	79
5.2	The three lines of defence model	82
5.3	Risk governance at group level	84
5.4	Risk management at divisional level	91
5.5	Risk function reporting lines	92
6.1	Management structure in DCMS, 2009	110
6.2	Risk management framework in DCMS	113
6.3	Core elements of the risk management process	113
6.4	Inherent risk matrix	117
6.5	Partners involved in DCMS strategic objective on culture, media and sport	121
7.1	Management structure in Birmingham City Council	133
7.2	Council-wide responsibilities for risk	138
7.3	Core elements of the risk management process	138
7.4	Risk/opportunity prioritization matrix	141
7.5	Planning framework	148
7.6	Responsibilities within the performance framework	149
7.7	Performance report	150
7.8	The performance management control loop	151
8.1	Integrating risk and performance management	162

List of tables

3.1	Risk categories	26
4.1	Geographic spread of operations	49
4.2	Key statistics	50
4.3	Business segments	54
4.4	Key performance indicators	59
5.1	RBS: key financial statistics	74
5.2	Committees supporting the group board	85
5.3	Main risk categories in RBS	88
6.1	Current sources of risk management guidance in central government	105
6.2	Common types of risk facing DCMS	114
6.3	Impact	116
6.4	Likelihood	116
6.5	Primary risk groups within DCMS	118
6.6	DCMS risk register	120
7.1	Likelihood	140
7.2	Impact	141
7.3	Risk register	144
7.4	Action plan	145
8.1	Case study context	157

List of boxes

2.1	King code of governance for South Africa	10
2.2	OECD principles of corporate governance	11
2.3	Dutch corporate governance code	11
2.4	Narrow versus broad definitions of internal control	16
2.5	Extracts from Lehman Brothers' annual report, 2007	17
2.6	Example of multi-layered governance system	18
3.1	Components of enterprise risk management	30
4.1	Process risk mapping for internal audit	64
4.2	Internal audit of overseas site acquisition	65
4.3	Monitoring of price risk: example	66
5.1	Internal control	77
5.2	Regulatory risk: example	87
6.1	Key statistics	107
6.2	Review of effectiveness, from the SIC of the DCMS, 2009	111
6.3	Partnership risk assurance	125
7.1	Key statistics, 2008–9	132
7.2	Training in risk identification and control	137
7.3	Example: library service	139

Acknowledgements

This book could not have been written without help from a wide range of people and organizations. I am particularly grateful to the Chartered Institute of Management Accountants (CIMA) for financial support, without which the underlying research would not have been possible. Additionally, I would like to thank both CIMA and the Institute of Risk Management (IRM) for their endorsement in the forewords. It is great that they believe the cases will be helpful to their students and members. Special thanks are also due to the many anonymous interviewees at each of the four organizations who were generous enough to give me many hours of their time. The case studies reflect my own interpretation of what I saw in each organization. I hope that the interviewees feel that the story I tell about risk management is an accurate reflection of the state of play in their organizations in the run up to the financial crisis.

A number of colleagues, most notably Kevin Dowd, Chris Humphrey, Chris O'Brien and associates from the European Risk Research Network such as Philip Linsley, Philip Shrives, Peter Kajüter and Paul Collier have also played an important part in helping me to develop the book.

Lastly, I would like to thank my family for putting up with my endless conversations about risk and for serving as a wonderfully balancing and supportive influence in my life.

Foreword (CIMA)

Over the last decade or so, there has been increasing recognition of the importance of an enterprise-wide approach to risk management in contributing to long-term sustainable success and coping with an uncertain and complex business environment. But what has really focused minds has been the global financial crisis which has represented the biggest and most damaging failure of corporate leadership of modern times. Commentators may have different views on the causes and remedies, but the need to manage risk better has been a recurrent and powerful theme.

It is no surprise therefore that enterprise risk management is right at the top of CIMA's thought leadership agenda. The case studies in this book are a direct outcome of our programme of sponsoring leading-edge research which generates high calibre and authoritative results that have immediate practical influence and value. You can find out more about our research on risk at www.cimaglobal.com/reportingandmanagingrisk. As the world's leading and largest professional body of management accountants, with 183,000 members and students in 168 countries, CIMA members and students work in industry, commerce and not for profit organisations. For all of them, risk management is an essential part of their toolkit.

The four case studies in the book are all based on interviews with key staff in the organisations and provide a snapshot of risk management at an important time for both the public and private sectors. If you are tempted to read just one case study on the argument that it's the one most relevant to the sector you work in, I would say 'resist'! That is because much of the interest comes from understanding how core principles of risk management – such as embedding risk management in a way that is consistent with the organisation's culture – have been applied in some very different environments.

Another key message is that while finance and risk management specialists still need to apply some of their traditional skills such as calculating value at risk (VaR), other softer skills such as influencing and communicating are increasingly important. What is very clear is that all organisations must avoid such traps as box-ticking approaches and getting lost in the complexity of sophisticated risk calculations. The ability to exercise considered and intelligent judgement is paramount.

At CIMA, we believe that case studies are excellent ways of sharing knowledge and practical insights so this book will make a valuable addition to any manager's bookshelf.

Charles Tilley
Chief Executive
Chartered Institute of Management Accountants (CIMA)

Foreword (IRM)

Although life in the twenty-first century is, for most people, longer, healthier and safer than ever before, uncertainty about the future is still an immutable feature of the business environment. This uncertainty has most recently demanded that we cope with financial crises, volcanic ash clouds, terrorist activity, strikes, cyber crime, energy insecurity and flu pandemics. But uncertainty also presents opportunities to be seized – developing markets, cheaper and better technology, global human connection via the Internet, medical advances and creative and artistic achievement. One person's risk, for example an asset price bubble, may also be another person's opportunity, depending on whether you're an investor in the stock market or the hedge fund.

All organisations, whatever their size and whatever their business, are under growing pressure to improve their understanding and management of the risks and opportunities that they face. Twenty years ago this responsibility would probably have been dealt with by a 'silo-based' approach: insurance would be purchased for the obvious insurable risks; the premises or site manager would look after health and safety; project managers would manage projects and the IT manager might have a disaster recovery plan. These departments would probably not see much need to talk to each other about risk, let alone to other departments like marketing, HR or accounts.

But a series of high profile corporate collapses and calamities, ranging from Enron to Woolworths to BP, has underlined that the old silo approach, while effective in its specialist parts, was not addressing the sort of risks that actually bring organisations to their knees. These risks tend to be messy, human, behavioural, complex and fiendishly interconnected, or maybe so completely unpredictable that they can only be addressed via a deliberately "holistic", "integrated" or "enterprise wide" approach. Enterprise risk management (or ERM) is now seen as an overarching board level concern and a critical factor in determining the organisation's long term success. The aim is not only to avoid losses, but also to provide competitive advantage, to take advantage of the opportunities offered by change, and to enhance reputation and value. The idea, as embodied in various risk management standards and guidance including the most recent ISO 31000, is relatively simple: what could stop (or assist) the organisation achieving its business objectives and what should be done about it. Real world execution however is rather more challenging.

With over 3,000 members around the world, the Institute of Risk Management is the leading educational body for the enterprise risk management profession. We believe strongly in the need to balance academic and theoretical approaches with practical, "hands on", tools and techniques and our qualifications and training are designed with this in mind. We believe that the case studies set out in this book, based on sound research and set firmly within the context of the most up to date governance and standards frameworks, make a real contribution to the understanding of risk management within organisations. At IRM we don't believe that there is a 'one size fits all' risk management solution – every organisation is different and must find an approach that works for its particular structure and culture – and this is demonstrated by the very different approaches, priorities and activities evident in the case study research. Our students and members are always asking for more real life examples and they now have an excellent additional resource to draw upon.

Steve Fowler
Chief Executive Officer
The Institute of Risk Management
www.theirm.org

Introduction

Sometimes it's the things you don't see that have the biggest impact.
(Enron advertisement, 2001 Media Guide for the Houston Astros baseball team)

In the light of Enron's subsequent bankruptcy and the more recent banking crisis, the words from this advertisement provide a succinct and highly apt justification for risk management. Enron and the banks have proved that risk management matters.

The fact that risk management is now a focus of attention for regulators, politicians, investors and the broader public can only be regarded as a good thing. At the same time, however, company directors and managers face the immediate challenge of how to ensure that they are exercising effective control over corporate risks whilst still taking advantage of the opportunities to expand and develop their businesses.

This book is aimed at the people who have day-to-day responsibility for risk management in an organization, or acting as advisers to such people. In addition, it is hoped that it will be useful for students taking courses in risk management, and perhaps considering a related career. The case studies, which form the core of the book, are intended to serve as illustrative examples of alternative approaches to risk management within some of the UK's major organizations. They highlight the fact that codes of governance and national/international standards for risk management merely provide a foundation stone upon which a risk management system can be constructed. The details and design of construction will differ between organizations because each one is different in terms of its objectives, size, culture and business model. Architectural design may appear to be a 'back office' function but it is fundamental to a building's success. Similarly, risk management is a critically important 'back office' function that can make or break a business.

While the case studies are diverse, the common messages are obvious, providing information and guidance for senior management, as well as offering lessons to risk managers who are seeking to make an enhanced contribution to the success of their employer. The importance of maintaining a risk aware culture is recognized in the new UK Corporate Governance Code and the components of a successful risk aware culture are described in this book. Also, the benefits of a well developed risk reporting structure (risk architecture) are explained, including the need to establish risk escalation procedures. Risk communication within risk architecture enables an organization to achieve a consistent and appropriate risk response. This approach will enable risk management activities to fully support the achievement of the strategic objectives of the organization.

The remainder of this book is structured as follows. The first chapter provides brief guidance on how to use the book, with the guidance differentiating between academic and practitioner users. Chapters 2 and 3 provide a historical context for the case studies. Chapter 1 details the link between risk and governance and outlines the historical development of governance regulation and its role in raising the profile of risk management. Chapter 3 explains the links and overlaps between risk management and internal control and provides a historical analysis of the development of risk management standards around the world. The chapter also includes discussion of the evolution of the role of the risk manager – its relationship to internal audit and the 'professionalization' of the function through the establishment of a range of different bodies and the creation of the role of Chief Risk Officer. The chapter clearly illustrates that risk management now extends well beyond the treasury and finance functions to encompass the broader concept of Enterprise Risk Management.

Chapters 4 to 7 contain the case studies, each of which forms a single chapter. The cases illustrate how four major UK organizations respond very differently to a common set of external influences that are driving the introduction of formalized risk management systems. The first case shows how the highly successful retailer Tesco PLC has been able to use risk management as a tool to improve its performance and overall business success. Case two, in contrast, highlights the ways in which failures of risk management were central to the problems faced by Royal Bank of Scotland during the 2007/8 financial crisis. The remaining two cases are based within the public sector and provide evidence that it is both simplistic and incorrect to assume that public sector management skills lag behind those of the private sector. Public sector bodies face highly complex and interdependent risks which are challenging to manage. Birmingham City Council has created mechanisms to link staff performance evaluation with responsibility for risks and in so doing it appears to be ahead of practice across much of the private sector. Similarly, whilst the DCMS recognizes that it still has a lot to learn about risk management, it uses relatively sophisticated mechanisms to manage partnership risks which again offer lessons for the private sector.

Chapter 8 reviews the overall story that emerges from the case studies and the possible lessons to be learnt, with a view to identifying the factors critical to success in developing an enterprise-wide risk management system. The issues covered include the impact of corporate culture on how risks are managed within an organization, and the extent to which risk remains a separate function as opposed to one which is integrated into the broader one of performance management. The chapter concludes that the key lesson from this book is that governance regulations and risk management standards are just a starting point. All risk management systems need to be sensitive to context and that means they will be individual to each organization. There remains, however, extensive scope for learning about best practice by sharing ideas and information across organizations.

1 How to use this book

The book can be used in a number of different ways:

- As a complete text.
- Study of individual chapters.
- Study of individual cases.

This flexibility allows for use by risk practitioners, university students (particularly postgraduate) and also those taking an executive development course. The guidance that follows offers some ideas on how the material in the book might be used by any/all of these groups in their search for improvements in risk management practice.

Guidance notes for academic use

Studying individual chapters. Each chapter is self-contained and can be used to complement a lecture(s) and/or a seminar on the same topic. At the same time, the parts of the book work to subdivide it into clear themes as follows:

- *Part I, Chapters 2–3.* The development of governance codes and risk management systems.
- *Part II, Chapters 4–5.* Risk management in practice: (1) the private sector.
- *Part III, Chapters 6–7.* Risk management in practice: (2) the public sector.
- *Part IV, Chapter 8.* Key lessons for the future, based on the content of Parts I and II.

For teaching use, the material in Part I may be useful for courses in accounting and business history as well as those in risk management. Similarly, post-experience courses or MBA modules might find that a combination of a single case from Part II or Part III together with elements of Chapter 8 from Part IV can be useful in driving discussion. Part IV also provides a central focus for any module which is analysing the origins and consequences of the financial crisis because it extends the debate beyond the purely banking issues into a broader management arena.

Using the case studies. The issues raised within each case differ because although the general regulatory and guidance frameworks on risk management are common across both the public and private sector, each organization has their own way of working and internal culture. For this reason, the cases may be studied independently or used in combination to draw out issues of similarities versus differences. Another possible use is comparison of just the private sector cases or comparison of the public versus private sector.

Every attempt has been made to ensure that the information included is as up to date as possible prior to publication, but where source material is publicly available, e.g., in company annual reports it is advisable for students to check if they can see any changes to the governance structures and systems detailed in the text.

Each case study concludes with a set of suggested questions for classroom discussion. In addition, more complex questions that link issues which cut across the cases are included in Chapter 8. This allows for a course to build up its level of complexity by starting with a single case and moving to comparative analysis at a later stage.

Guidance notes for practitioner use

Part I. This material provides a background to the development of risk management and so may be useful in preparing for professional examinations in this field. The content may also be used selectively to construct training material on, for example, what is meant by ERM, or the core components of a risk management system. Similarly, it can provide a starting point for risk identification by managers.

Parts II–III. The case studies contain a wealth of material that can be used to provide a basis for:

- Critical comment upon alternative models of governance and risk management.
- Comparison of one's own organization's approach with that of one or more case study organizations.
- Discussion of a single issue of significance to your particular organization e.g. how to manage partnership risk or how to comply with regulations without falling into a silo-based, compliance-oriented mind set.

Part IV. The discussion in Chapter 8, which compares the different cases, draws out the challenges of implementing ERM in terms of getting support for risk management across the whole of an organization. For practitioners this raises many questions such as:

- Does our business model affect our exposure to risk and if so how?
- What is the difference between risk management and compliance?
- How can we rank and prioritize risks?

- What systems need to be established to ensure risks are reported effectively to both internal management and external stakeholders?
- Is our risk system focused upon compliance of corporate objectives?
- Do we want an ERM based model of risk management in our organization and if so why?
- What time frame are we anticipating being required for it to reach maturity, defined as when risk based thinking is integrated across the whole organization?
- How frequently should we review progress in relation to ERM implementation?
- To what extent do we believe that risk and performance are inextricably linked, and do our control systems reflect that view? If they do not, what changes need to be made?

Part I

Governance and risk management

2 Risk and governance

Aim

The aim of this chapter is to briefly review the recent history of risk management and governance regulation in order to illustrate:

- The link between risk management and corporate governance.
- That the historical development of governance regulations post-2002 has served to significantly raise the profile of risk management.
- The ongoing global emphasis on 'light' regulation of risk management and internal control.
- The need to recognize that compliance with governance regulations offers only limited assurance that risks are being managed effectively.

The conclusion that compliance with governance regulations does not necessarily translate into good risk management provides a backdrop for the case studies which follow, as they illustrate how regulations are interpreted in practice within companies to create different types of risk culture, with varying degrees of effectiveness.

Risk management and corporate governance

The UK Corporate Governance Code (FRC, 2010, p. 1) describes the purpose of corporate governance as being 'to facilitate effective, entrepreneurial and prudent management that can deliver the long-term success of the company'. The Code takes the view that a company's board of directors is 'collectively responsible for the long-term success of the company' (FRC, 2010, p. 6). The Board's duties in this regard include responsibility for determining the nature and extent of the significant risks it is willing to take in achieving its strategic objectives and the maintenance of 'sound risk management and internal control systems'.

In other words, risk management is a component of corporate governance. Boxes 2.1–3 illustrate how this view is echoed across governance codes throughout the rest of the world. The link between risk and governance is also widely recognized within the academic literature. Spira and Page (2003) suggest that in the process of becoming central to corporate governance the meaning of the term 'risk' has evolved, as risks are now managed through a framework of accountability which encompasses financial reporting, internal control and audit. The emphasis on accountability is important because it can be argued that demands for increased accountability lie at the heart of the development of worldwide governance and risk management regulations, codes and standards over the last 20 years. Additionally, the gradual redefinition of internal control as 'risk management' has worked to the benefit of certain groups and the growing professionalization of risk management. This issue is discussed in more depth in Chapter 3.

Two phases of regulatory change

Phase one: 1990–2000

In the UK, a series of corporate scandals in the early 1990s – Polly Peck (1990), BCCI (1991) and the Maxwell Group pensions affair (1991) served to damage confidence in financial reporting and generate demands for increased managerial accountability. Some years earlier (1985), the Committee on Sponsoring Organizations (COSO) had been founded in the United States. COSO was established to sponsor the National Commission on Fraudulent Financial Reporting – commonly referred to as the Treadway Commission (after its first chairman).

Box 2.1 King Code of Governance for South Africa (2009)

> Good governance is essentially about effective *leadership*. ... Responsible leaders direct company strategies and operations with a view to achieving sustainable economic, social and environmental performance.
>
> (Institute of Directors in Southern Africa 2009, p. 9).

As part of its duties in relation to governance, the board carries responsibility for the governance of risk and recommended practice is as follows:

- A policy and plan for a system and process of risk management should be developed.
- The board should comment in the integrated report on the effectiveness of the system and process of risk management.
- The board's responsibility for risk governance should be expressed in the board charter.
- The induction and ongoing training programmes the board should incorporate.

Box 2.2 OECD Principles of Corporate Governance (2004)

The corporate governance framework should ensure the strategic guidance of the company, the effective monitoring of management by the board, and the board's accountability to the company and the shareholders.

(p.24)

The board should fulfil certain key functions, including:

Ensuring the integrity of the corporation's accounting and financial reporting systems, including the independent audit, and that appropriate systems of control are in place, in particular, systems for risk management, financial and operational control, and compliance with the law and relevant standards.

(p.25)

Box 2.3 Dutch corporate governance code (2009)

The management board and the supervisory board are responsible for the corporate governance structure of the company and for compliance with this code. They are accountable for this to the general meeting and should provide sound reasons for any non-application of the provisions.

(p.11)

The role of the management board is to manage the company, which means, among other things, that it is responsible for achieving the company's aims, the strategy and associated risk profile, the development of results and corporate social responsibility issues that are relevant to the enterprise. The management board is accountable for this to the supervisory board and to the general meeting.

(p.11)

The management board is responsible for complying with all relevant primary and secondary legislation, for managing the risks associated with the company activities and for financing the company. The management board shall report related developments to and shall discuss the internal risk management and control systems with the supervisory board and the audit committee.

(p.12)

The commission was sponsored by five major professional associations headquartered in the United States: the American Accounting Association (AAA), the American Institute of Certified Public Accountants (AICPA), Financial Executives International (FEI), The Institute of Internal Auditors (IIA) and the National Association of Accountants (now the Institute of Management Accountants, IMA) with the remit of looking at the causes underlying fraudulent financial reporting.

This consciousness of a need for greater confidence in financial reporting started the first decade of governance initiatives, which began with the publication of the first major internal control framework by COSO in 1992. The COSO framework (p. 3) defined internal control as 'a process, effected by an entity's board of directors, management and other personnel, designed to provide reasonable assurance regarding the achievement of objectives' in the following categories:

- Effectiveness and efficiency of operations.
- Reliability of financial reporting.
- Compliance with applicable laws and regulations.

The COSO report defined internal control as being made up of five interrelated components:

- Control environment.
- Risk assessment.
- Control activities.
- Information and communication.
- Monitoring.

These five components should not be viewed as discrete elements, but as connected mechanisms that work in combination to provide assurance about the three core objectives.

Detailed definitions of each of the component elements of the framework can be found within the COSO document, but risk assessment is of particular interest in the context of this book. Most important, the 1992 version of COSO positioned risk assessment as a sub-element of a broader internal control framework aimed at providing assurance to stakeholders. As the next section shows, however, by the time a revised version of COSO was issued in 2004 this view had been revised in a way that significantly raised the profile of risk management.

The wording used in the COSO definition of internal control is echoed in other subsequent governance frameworks, including the *Criteria of Control Board Guidance on Control* (CoCO), issued in Canada in 1995 and the Turnbull *Guidance for Directors on the Combined Code*, published in the UK in 1999. The common theme that links all of these frameworks is the idea that internal control processes provide a mechanism through which management can provide assurance regarding the pursuit and achievement of corporate objectives.

In COSO, each category of objective requires that all five components are present, and this is most effectively achieved when the controls are built in to the organizational infrastructure such that control is not a separate consideration, but is instead a part of the 'essence' of the business. Similarly, in Turnbull the view is clearly expressed that internal control should be embedded within the normal management processes of a business rather than being seen as a separate exercise undertaken to ensure regulatory compliance. CoCo confirms the idea that 'internal control is integral to the activities of the company, and not something practiced [*sic*] in remote corners' (IFAC, 2006). From a governance perspective, the idea of controls which are embedded is hugely important. From an empirical perspective, however, this embedding is very difficult to achieve.

One of the recurring themes in this book is the extent to which internal controls – and more specifically risk management – can become divorced from the operational realities of a business. The risk management function can become wrapped up in dealing with issues of compliance and be isolated in silos so that it has little direct contact with day-to-day operations and holds little meaning for front-line staff. The case studies reveal very different corporate mindsets in relation to this important issue and show that embedding risk management into operations is an extremely challenging and long term process.

In summary, the phase of regulatory change from 1990–2000 is characterized by the publication of the first sets of guidelines on internal control and corporate governance. In chronological order, the key ones include COSO, 1992 (United States), CoCo, 1995 (Canada), the Peter's Committee Report (Netherlands), 1997, and Turnbull, 1999 (UK). The decade also saw the publication of the world's first standard on risk management (AS/NZS, 4360: 1995), in Australia and New Zealand. By 2000, therefore, the foundations were in place for similar codes and standards to be developed in other countries and also for the existing governance and control frameworks to be refined and extended.

Laying the foundations for governance does not, however, guarantee widespread adoption of the suggested practices. There is useful, but rather limited, evidence on the extent to which COSO 1992 was adopted by US companies. A 1996 survey of 300 senior executives and 200 non-management employees conducted by Coopers and Lybrand and cited by Gupta (2006) found very limited take-up of the COSO model, with only 10 per cent of executives saying they were even aware of its existence (Drake and Sever, 1996). The implication is that 'COSO 1992 was more of a philosophical treatise written by a group of accountants to draw the attention of C suite executives to the concept of internal control as a fundamentally sound business practice' (Gupta, 2006, p. 59). The position changed rather dramatically over the course of the next ten years.

Phase two: 2000–2010

More scandals

Despite the governance reforms outlined above, the early years of the new millennium were marked by a spate of corporate scandals and malfeasance. The energy trading company Enron collapsed in late 2001 amidst an accounting scandal that triggered comments that it was a 'virtual company earning virtual profits'. The Enron scandal triggered a spate of both accounting and governance reforms, at the centre of which was the Sarbanes Oxley Act of 2002 (SOX), described by President Bush as 'the most far reaching reforms of American business practices since the time of Franklin Delano Roosevelt'.

Whilst the Enron story was still unfolding and SOX still awaiting enactment, the Bermuda-based telecommunications company Global Crossing filed for Chapter 11 bankruptcy in January 2001 amidst accusations of artificially inflated profits. Shortly afterwards, in the same month that SOX became law, WorldCom filed for Chapter 11 bankruptcy in what at the time was the largest such filing in US corporate history. Many major US banks, including J. P. Morgan Chase, Citibank, Goldman Sachs and Credit Suisse First Boston were highly exposed to Worldcom, and listed amongst the 50 largest creditors named in the filing,

The introduction of SOX thus marked what many hoped might be a move away from a low point in US corporate and financial history. The key question was, would it provide an assurance regime that ensured financial scandals would be consigned to history? Whilst the act was subject to much criticism, there were also very many who hoped that it might mark the start of a new period of improved governance and disclosure. Unfortunately, however, the 2007–8 banking crisis proved this to be a rather short lived hope. To understand the limitations of SOX, and why it did not prevent the banking crisis, it is helpful to look more closely at the detail of the legislation, because it is in the detail that we discover problems with the definition of the terms risk management and internal control.

Sarbanes Oxley Act 2002

The Act mandated a number of reforms to enhance corporate responsibility and financial disclosures and combat corporate and accounting fraud. Amongst these reforms was the creation of the Public Company Accounting Oversight Board, or PCAOB, to oversee the activities of the auditing profession.

Solomon and Peecher (2004) argue that SOX sought to protect investors, shareholders and creditors from the breakdowns in internal control that result in financial disasters, and as such it clearly revisited the aims that underpinned the Foreign Corrupt Practices Act (FCPA) of 1977. SOX affirmed that the FCPA had been insufficiently effective in ensuring the reliability of public financial reporting and directly linked the reliability of financial statements to the maintenance of effective internal control systems.

Sections 302 and 404 of SOX are amongst the most controversial requirements of the Act. Under Section 404, a company's annual filing with the Securities and Exchange Commission (SEC) is required to include an internal control report which not only acknowledges management's responsibility for establishing and maintaining an adequate internal control structure and procedures for financial reporting but also includes an assessment of the effectiveness of those internal controls attested by the external auditors. Under SEC rules on the implementation of Section 404, the assessment (including testing) must be supported by reasonable evidential matter.

Section 302, complements Section 404 in requiring the company's executives to certify that they have undertaken an evaluation of the effectiveness of their internal controls over financial reporting and where the controls are classified as not effective, they must disclose any material weaknesses that have been identified.

So how is control effectiveness assessed? The SEC rules indicated that effectiveness can be demonstrated through provision of evidence that a suitable internal control framework is in place. The COSO 1992 guidelines are one example of a 'suitable framework' (SEC, 2006, p. 5), with the Canadian 'CoCo' guidance and the UK's Turnbull Guidance serving as suitable alternatives. Not surprisingly, therefore, one consequence of SOX was that COSO 1992 rapidly became the dominant model for internal control design amongst US companies.

COSO 1992 remained the dominant model for internal control design until the framework was redrafted in 2004 and retitled 'Enterprise Risk Management – Integrated Framework' (COSO, 2004). Since 2004 it is this version which is most commonly used to assess compliance with SOX. It might seem a mere technicality that the framework was updated, but the changes that were incorporated served to significantly raise the profile of risk management. In effect, the 2004 version reversed the relative importance of risk management and internal control, as the former was renamed 'enterprise risk management', a term 'that incorporates the internal control framework within it' (COSO, 2004, foreword, p. v). These changes have impacted heavily on both the risk and the audit professions.

The banking crisis

The preceding discussion highlights the linkage between the development of US rules and legislation on corporate governance and the growth in importance of the concept of risk management. Nonetheless, the first decade of the century is drawing to a close with companies and nations around the world struggling to recover from a banking crisis which originated in the United States. What is more, there are few commentators who do not blame poor governance within the financial institutions for the crisis. Extended debate on the causes of the financial crisis are beyond the scope of this book, but it is nonetheless important to consider the governance and risk management dimensions of the problems which hits the world's banks.

Perhaps the most obvious observation on the crisis is that the shortcomings in corporate governance occurred in spite of the existence of well developed regulatory frameworks. This suggests that *existence* and *effectiveness* of internal control and risk management systems do not necessarily coincide, either at national or institutional levels. Reporting that you have complied with a particular governance code, and saying you have reviewed the control system does not mean that it is actually working effectively. Furthermore, if the boundaries of the control system (for regulatory purposes) are tightly defined, as in SOX, then the controls outside that boundary may also be potentially ineffective.

The scope for contradiction between perception and reality in terms of risk management and internal control can be usefully illustrated by reference to the failed US bank Lehman Brothers. In September 2008 Lehman Brothers filed for bankruptcy despite the fact that in its Annual Report, for 2007 Lehman described their approach to risk management as follows: 'While risk cannot be eliminated, it can be mitigated to the greatest extent possible through a strong internal control environment. Essential in our approach to risk management is a strong internal control environment with multiple overlapping and reinforcing elements'.

The extracts clearly show that both the bank's executives and their auditors believed that the internal controls over financial reporting were effective, but it was not bad reporting that led to the bankruptcy – it was poor management of broader-based business risks. In other words, compliance with regulation offers an incomplete form of assurance. A 2008 report by the Institute of Chartered Secretaries and Administrators noted that many companies treat governance as 'a compilation of rules and regulations which add little value' (Skypala, 2008).

The case studies in this book illustrate that governance regulations and risk management standards and rules merely provide a skeleton on which the flesh of a control system can be overlaid and used in practice. The underlying skeleton or bone structure may be identical across different organizations but the resulting internal control system will reflect individual traits, linked to the business model, corporate culture and management style. Consequently, it can be argued that on a stand alone basis, the value added by standards and regulations is minimal – the real value is added by the way that they are used in practice to ensure the achievement of organizational objectives.

Box 2.4 Narrow versus broad definitions of internal control

SOX only talks about internal control in terms of the controls relating to financial reporting. In other words it seeks only to provide assurance about the reliability of financial reporting. In practice firms are open to a much broader range of risks and require a much broader set of internal controls which encompass the full range of company activities and extend well beyond financial issues.

The King Code (2009, p.8) is critical of the approach taken in SOX and notes that ' SOX – with all of its statutory requirements for rigorous internal controls – has not prevented the collapse of many of the leading names in US banking and finance.

Box 2.5 Extracts from Lehman Bros' Annual Report, 2007

Management's assessment of internal control over financial reporting

The Company's management assessed the effectiveness of the Company's internal control over financial reporting as of November 30, 2006. In making this assessment, it used the criteria set forth by the Committee of Sponsoring Organizations of the Treadway Commission (COSO) in *Internal Control – Integrated Framework*. Based on our assessment we believe that, as of November 30, 2006, the Company's internal control over financial reporting is effective based on those criteria.

(p.68)

Report of independent registered public accounting firm on internal control over financial reporting

We have audited management's assessment, included in the accompanying *Management's Assessment of Internal Control over Financial Reporting*, that Lehman Brothers Holdings Inc. (the 'Company') maintained effective internal control over financial reporting as of November 30, 2006, based on criteria established in Internal Control – Integrated Framework issued by the Committee of Sponsoring Organizations of the Treadway Commission (the COSO criteria).

We conducted our audit in accordance with the standards of the Public Company Accounting Oversight Board (United States). Those standards require that we plan and perform the audit to obtain reasonable assurance about whether effective internal control over financial reporting was maintained in all material respects. Our audit included obtaining an understanding of internal control over financial reporting, evaluating management's assessment, testing and evaluating the design and operating effectiveness of internal control, and performing such other procedures as we considered necessary in the circumstances. We believe that our audit provides a reasonable basis for our opinion.

In our opinion, management's assessment that the Company maintained effective internal control over financial reporting as of November 30, 2006, is fairly stated, in all material respects, based on the COSO criteria. Also, in our opinion, the Company maintained, in all material respects, effective internal control over financial reporting as of November 30, 2006, based on the COSO criteria (p.69).

'Hard' versus 'soft' laws of governance

The Sarbanes Oxley Act is an example of management of governance regimes via statute, but such an approach can face problems. It was not long before criticisms of SOX began to emerge, and these were focused largely around the costs incurred by companies in ensuring compliance. The arguments suggested that the regulations in SOX are:

- *A form of hidden taxation.*
- *Economically inefficient.* It is estimated that the total cost to the US economy of implementing SOX equates to US$1.4 trillion, compared with total losses of US$427 billion from the major scandals of Enron, WorldCom, Tyco and Global Crossing.
- *Damaging to the attractiveness of the US markets to foreign listings.* In a speech in 2006 Alan Greenspan said he was 'acutely aware and disturbed' by the shift in Initial Public Offerings away from the United States and towards London as a result of SOX.

Perhaps in recognition of such criticisms, the governance of corporations on a statutory basis remains largely confined to the United States. The UK, together with the 56 countries of the British Commonwealth and 27 states in the EU, have all opted for a code of principles and practices based on a 'comply or explain' basis (King Code, 2009), complemented by a limited number of governance issues that are the subject of legislation. The precise terminology differs a little from place to place – for example in the UN Governance Code it is 'adopt or explain' and in the Netherlands it is 'apply or explain' – but the underlying principle of voluntary adoption is common across many countries.

To date, there is not full international convergence in the field of corporate governance and internal control, but there are strong moves in this direction. Within Europe, the European Corporate Governance Forum was set up by the Commission in October 2004. It is a committee of 15 members meeting every

---

Box 2.6 Example of multi layered governance system: the UK

The corporate governance framework in the UK operates at a number of levels:

- Through legislation particularly the Companies Act.
- Through regulations, such as the London Stock Exchange listing rules.
- Through the Combined Code which is the responsibility of the Financial Reporting Council.

four to six months, charged with examining best practice in EU Member States with a view to facilitating convergence of national corporate governance codes. A recent report on the adoption of 'comply or explain' codes with the 27 EU member states concluded that:

> the comply-or-explain approach formally adopted by the European Commission in 2006 enjoys wide acceptance by the corporate as well the institutional investor community ... However, its practical implementation suffers some deficiencies, mainly in the form of an unsatisfactory level and quality of information on deviations by companies and a low level of shareholder monitoring. These issues could be remedied ... and the comply-or-explain regime should not be abandoned. It should be strengthened.

(EU, 2008, p. 18)

Conclusion

In this chapter we have looked at the way in which the regulations and codes relating to corporate governance, internal control and risk management have developed concurrently. Governance codes from around the world have a number of common features which define internal controls as mechanisms or processes which help provide stakeholders with assurance that an organization is pursuing and achieving its objectives.

The chapter divides the history of the development of governance regulations into two key time periods, 1990–2000 and 2000–10. The first period laid down the initial codes of governance, which were refined and extended in the second period. In both decades, major corporate scandals served as triggers for regulation. Initially, the desire was for greater confidence in financial reporting, but when the Enron crisis struck the United States in late 2001/early 2002 it was decided that further legislation was required and the Sarbanes Oxley Act was subsequently passed. The regulations in SOX were closely linked to the COSO framework for internal control, which was itself revised in 2004. This linkage served to both reaffirm the idea that internal control is fundamental to good governance but also to simultaneously raise the profile of risk management. COSO 2004 placed enterprise risk management as the overall control system, within which other internal controls had a subsidiary place. Despite the new and seemingly tighter governance regulations, however, the global banking crisis struck in 2007.

The crisis revealed stark failures of governance within some of the world's largest banks, and in so doing it also highlighted the fact that the SOX legislation, which covered only internal controls over financial reporting, missed the case for strong internal controls over the broader spread of business activity. Additionally, the crisis clearly showed that legislation and codes are not all that is required to ensure good governance. Professor Michael Power of LSE goes even further commenting that 'the financial crisis suggests an urgent need to shift cognitive and economic resources from "rule-based compliance" towards the "critical imagination of alternative futures" (Power, 2009, p. 852)'. Internal cultures within organizations and the resulting attitudes towards risk taking are clearly very important. This idea is perhaps reflected in the concept of 'comply or explain' governance codes, as opposed to legally based governance systems. 'Comply or explain' serves to transfer responsibility across to companies to choose to adopt given standards of control. Even so, banks operating within such regimes encountered problems within the crisis.

All of this suggests that ultimately the quality of governance is a matter for the individual organization. No amount of legislation can force good governance if there is a lack of local willingness to engage with the underlying principles. As a result, the approach to governance and more specifically to risk management will vary from organization to organization, even in the context of common sets of regulations. The case studies reveal this most clearly and provide useful lessons for those aiming to raise their standards of governance.

References

Committee of Sponsoring Organizations of the Treadway Commission (COSO) (1992) *Internal Control – Integrated Framework*, Jersey City, NJ: American Institute of Certified Public Accountants.

Committee of Sponsoring Organizations of the Treadway Commission (2004) *Enterprise Risk Management*, New York, NY: AICPA.

Drake, K. and Sever, J. (1996) *The Coopers & Lybrand Survey of Internal Control in Corporate America: A Report on what Corporations are and are not Doing to Manage Risks*, New York: Louis Harris & Associates.

(FRC) Financial Reporting Council (2010) *UK Corporate Governance Code*, http://www.frc.org.uk/documents/pagemanager/Corporate_Governance/UK%20Corp%20Gov%20Code%20June%202010.pdf

Gupta, P. (2006) *Internal Control: COSO 1992 Control Framework and Management Reporting on Internal Control: Survey and Analysis of Implementation Practices*, Montvale, NJ: IMA.

Institute of Directors in Southern Africa (2009) *King Code of Governance for South Africa*, http://www.iodsa.co.za/downloads/documents/King_Code_2009.pdf

OECD (2004) *Principles of Corporate Governance*, http://www.oecd.org/dataoecd/32/18/31557724.pdf

Power, M. (2009) 'The risk management of nothing', *Accounting, Organizations and Society*, Vol. 34, pp. 849–55.

Skypala, P. (2008) 'Time to reward good corporate governance', *ft.com*, 18 November, http://www.ft.com/cms/s/0/a308a71e-b275-11dd-bbc9-0000779fd18c.html

Solomon, I. and Peecher, M. (2004) 'SOS 404: a billion here, a billion there', *Wall Street Journal*, Managers' Journal, 9 November.

Spira, L. and Page, M. (2003) 'Risk management: the reinvention of internal control and the changing role of internal audit', *Accounting, Auditing and Accountability Journal*, Vol. 16, No. 4, pp. 640–61.

Useful web links

- http://www.sarbanes-oxley-forum.com/. This forum includes many links to discussion threads and comments about the act as well as providing access to a downloadable PDF version Sarbanes Oxley Act 2002.
- http://ec.europa.eu/internal_market/company/ecgforum/index_en.htm. This is the home page of the European Corporate Governance Forum and is a useful site to gain more information about European initiatives in this area, including a study on 'comply or explain'.

Discussion questions

1   Suggest examples of situations in (a) your daily living and (b) your work life where strong emphasis is placed on compliance with rules. Use these examples to discuss the extent to which the rules are being used to help achieve sensible and clearly articulated objectives, or as a cushion to protect against accusations of failure. In preparation for this it may help to review the ideas of Michael Power on how modern society seems to be characterized by people checking up on each other, demanding accountability and monitoring risk. Look at Chapter 6 in his book *The Audit Society Rituals of Verification* (1997).
2   Analyse the governance structure of your own organization (or one of your choice) and look at the extent to which it tries to link controls back to the organizational objectives. Are there any missing elements? Could the governance structure be improved at all, and if so how?

3 Risk and control

Aim

The aim of this chapter is to discuss the linkages between risk management and control. By discussing the benefits of risk categorization and how national and international standards and codes of practice have evolved, the chapter explains how organizations today can access a standardized framework for risk management which complements the governance frameworks described in Chapter 2. In addition, the chapter argues that such standardization, especially as expressed through the concept of Enterprise Risk Management (ERM), remains idealized. Evidence suggests that it is proving extraordinarily challenging to implement ERM in practice. Furthermore, the increasing level of attention being paid to risk management has resulted in a variety of different professional bodies competing for the risk 'space' by arguing that they are best equipped to address the issues. The chapter concludes that risk management frameworks in every organization have common features (based around the standards) but lines of responsibility are variable. This conclusion is reflected in the case studies which follow.

The chapter is broken into the following sections:

- Risk categories.
- Standards for risk management and Enterprise Risk Management.
- Who is responsible for risk management?

Risk categories

The ISO guide to risk management vocabulary defines risk as 'as the combination of the probability of an event and its consequences' (ISO Guide 73). The definition incorporates both opportunities (upside risk) and threats (downside risk), and risk management is thus concerned with providing mechanisms through which to control the impact of both the positive and negative aspects of risk.

Such a broad definition, however, hides a mass of complexity. Organizations face a multitude of different types of risk, which also change and evolve over time. As Tom Peters observed over twenty years ago, the business environment is characterized by 'unprecedented uncertainty' (Peters, 1989) and in such an environment people search for ways of managing that uncertainty. One starting point for doing so is to classify risks into categories, whilst recognizing that certain categories will have varying degrees of relevance according to the business sector within which an organization operates.

In a survey of senior executives from around the world, the Economist Intelligence Unit (EIU, 2005) asked respondents to rank different categories of risk on a scale of 1–100 in terms of their significance to their business. The survey results are summarized in Figure 3.1. As Figure 3.1 clearly shows, *reputation risk* is ranked top, but the EIU also reported that senior managers find it particularly difficult to manage. Reputation is a prized asset, but it could be argued that it is not a separate risk category in its own right, but instead merely reflects a failure to manage other risks. This idea is easily illustrated by reference to the reputational damage felt by BP as a result of the massive oil spill in the Gulf of Mexico in 2010. The company's reputation – and finances – were severely hit, but the explanations for the oil spill suggest a range of possible underlying causes (or risks), including BP's choice of construction contractors, operational controls, and the quality of material used in constructing the rig.

Reputation risk is therefore best viewed as a high level risk, but one which reflects the quality of control over other, lower level risks. Problems can escalate and ultimately impact upon a company's reputation. Reputation risk is vitally important, because for private organizations, reputation is a key driver of the business value. The erosion of reputation can damage future revenue streams and hence profitability, but reputation risks are high, because as Warren Buffett observed, 'It takes twenty years to build a reputation and five minutes

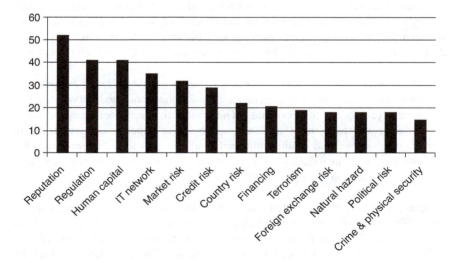

Figure 3.1 Risk rankings by category

Source: Adapted from Economist Intelligence Unit, 2005

to destroy it'. Preserving a company's reputation is therefore a very important dimension of risk management and there is evidence to suggest that it not only affects customers' buying decisions but also employee loyalty and investor choices. As such a good reputation can also serve as a barrier to entry and protect competitive position.

In the EIU survey, regulation risk comes out as the second most important risk for managers, reflecting the globalization of business and the associated complexity of ensuring full compliance with laws and regulations across a wide range of jurisdictions. For example, Coca-Cola HBC, just one of the Coca-Cola Group's European subsidiaries, operates across 26 different countries and needs risk management systems that are able to track compliance with a wide array of regulations across this whole area. HSBC, Europe's largest bank, faced problems in 2010 when the US Office of the Comptroller of the Currency issued an order against the bank's US subsidiary for violating a law governing how the company reports and assesses suspicious activity around its accounts, including international wire transfers and large cash withdrawals (Reuters, 2010). The regulators have not fined HSBC but have not precluded such an option in the future, and HSBC's board of directors must submit a plan to the Federal Reserve within 30 days, showing how it proposes to improve its compliance with anti-money laundering regulations. In similar vein, in August 2010, Barclays Bank agreed to pay $298 million to settle criminal charges that it violated US sanctions through dealings with banks in Cuba, Iran, Libya, Sudan and Myanmar (Reuters, 2010). These examples illustrate that failure to comply with regulation can be very damaging to a business.

Human capital also ranks high on the list of risks. The terms encompass elements such as the risk of facing shortages of essential skilled personnel, loss of key staff, and the need to manage the process of succession in critical roles within the organization. The sports goods business Nike provide a succinct description of this risk in their 2010 20K report to the SEC in which they state:

> *We depend on key personnel, the loss of whom would harm our business.*
> Our future success will depend in part on the continued service of key executive officers and personnel. The loss of the services of any key individual could harm us. Our future success also depends on our ability to identify, attract and retain additional qualified personnel. Competition for employees in our industry is intense and we may not be successful in attracting and retaining such personnel.

IT Risk arises because IT systems are now fundamental to most business processes. There are obvious cases, such as online retailers, who face the risk of massive loss of income if their ordering systems go down, or are accessed illegally. Less obviously, but equally significant, are the problems that may be caused, for example, by IT failure within a bank which may result in the failure of its electronic banking services. Similarly the risks associated with the loss of confidential data or frauds are substantially increased in environments that are heavily IT dependent.

It is difficult in practice to distinguish at times between IT risks and the broader category of *supply chain risks*. Failures in the supply chain – either backward facing in terms of suppliers, or forward facing towards consumers can be disastrous for organizations. One example of this is the domino effect caused by the collapse of the Woolworth retailing group in December 2008. When Entertainment UK (EUK), part of the group's distribution arm, went into administration, it left other retailers facing massive supply problems. Zavvi, which formerly traded as Virgin Megastores, was forced to call in help from Ernst and Young when it faced a massive cash flow problem in the run up to Christmas, because it had run out of CDs and DVDs which it had expected to receive from Entertainment UK, its main supplier.

For manufacturing organizations, market success is strongly linked to having an effective distribution network and risks in this area are therefore well recognized, as illustrated by another excerpt from the Nike 2010 report cited on page 24:

> *Our success depends on our global distribution facilities.*
> We distribute our products to customers directly from the factory and through distribution centers located throughout the world. Our ability to meet customer expectations, manage inventory, complete sales and achieve objectives for operating efficiencies depends on the proper operation of our distribution facilities, the development or expansion of additional distribution capabilities, and the timely performance of services by third parties (including those involved in shipping product to and from our distribution facilities). Our distribution facilities could be interrupted by information technology problems and disasters such as earthquakes or fires. Any significant failure in our distribution facilities could result in an adverse affect on our business. We maintain business interruption insurance, but it may not adequately protect us from adverse effects that could be caused by significant disruptions in our distribution facilities.

The remaining risks identified in Figure 3.1 encompass a mix of factors. Several fall under a general heading of financial risks – such as market risk (changes in market conditions), credit risk and foreign exchange risk, and there are plenty of tools that can be used to help manage these risks. Other categories, such as country risk, political risk or terrorism reflect factors which may be controllable to a lesser degree, but are nonetheless important.

The breakdown used by the EIU is just one example of how risks may be categorized, and perhaps too complex to be particularly useful. Grouping risks under a smaller number of common headings is a practice widely used by organizations as it enables senior management to see that several risks may originate from common sources or be managed in similar ways. One of the most common groupings that is in common use splits risks down under the following headings:

- Financial risks, e.g. liquidity risk; credit risk; financing risk; cash flow risk.

- Operational risks – these may arise from failures in products, by people or in processes. e.g. fraud; IT system failure; component failure; equipment breakdown; design flaws.
- Environmental risks – these are caused by factors external to the organization e.g. economic conditions; natural disasters; regulation; political change; climate change.

Many types of risk in each of these groupings will be faced by all organizations, regardless of their sector or size. Nonetheless, the way in which each organization categorizes and groups its risks and the relative importance attached to each of the categories will ultimately depend upon both the nature of the business and the level of detail sought by risk managers. The aim of classification is to begin the process of creating a framework which can be used to manage risks and the framework reported by Marks and Spencer, the UK retailer, is illustrated in Table 3.1. Note that this is based upon the information included within the governance section of the annual report and as such it may not exactly match the risk categorizations used internally to manage the business. The case studies contain more detail on *internally* generated risk categorizations.

Establishing a set of risk categories, or groups, that need to be managed allows an organization to clarify the issues to take into account in beginning to build a risk management system. Creating a more formal structure for the system is then done by making use of one of the many risk management standards which are now published. In the next section we see that whilst many countries have published their own standards, they possess many common features and this

Table 3.1 Risk categories

Risk category	Types of risk included
Strategy and finance	Economic outlook Competition Financial position
Brand and reputation	Brand and reputation, including failure to meet stakeholder commitments
People and change	Failure to attract, develop and retain key employees Failure to deliver major change projects with minimal disruption
Day-to-day operation	Stock management IT security Suppliers/third parties Supply chain
Selling channels	M&S Direct: failure to compete and grow business International: failure to leverage platforms and grow the business through a variety of entry modes

Source: Adapted from Marks & Spencer, Annual Report (2010), pp. 56–7

consistency has recently been formally recognized in the publication in 2009 of ISO 31000 *Risk Management – principles and guidelines.*

Standards for risk management and enterprise risk management

The UK's Risk Management Standard, published in 2002, argues that standards are needed to ensure that there is an agreed:

- Terminology related to the words used.
- Process by which risk management can be carried out.
- Organization structure for risk management.
- Objective for risk management.

In other words, standards provide tools that are helpful for both private and public sector organizations seeking to establish their own risk management systems. The declared intention is not to be prescriptive and encourage a box-ticking approach but simply to provide a mechanism through which organizations can check that they are compliant.

The point raised above is central to a key question of this book: what is the purpose of a risk management system? If risk management exists solely in order to ensure regulatory compliance, it may not be serving its full purpose and providing maximum benefit to an organization. If it exists to focus on managing any risks which may impede the achievement of organizational objectives then its function extends beyond merely that of compliance. The case studies in Chapters 4–7 clearly show the organizational impact of different risk mindsets, and demonstrate that a box-ticking mentality can be dangerous and lead to risks being missed. In other words, a compliance focused approach can cause both financial and reputational damage.

What standards exist?

It is neither useful nor feasible to try and cover all of the various national and international standards in this chapter. Instead, this section summarizes the overlapping approaches outlined within the Enterprise Risk Management (ERM) framework published in 2004 by the Committee of Sponsoring Organizations (COSO) and the global standard ISO 31000 (2009).

Background to ISO 31000 – risk management: principles and guidelines

The world's first risk management standard, AS/NSZ 4360, was issued jointly by Standards Australia and New Zealand in 1995, and subsequently revised in 1999 and 2004. It not only provided a basis used by other countries to develop their own standards, but also established a framework for the implementation of risk management approaches in a wide range of organizations. Over the course of the last decade the global integration of businesses, combined with a growing desire to develop and implement consistent risk management processes across the globe, led to recognition of the need for an international standard. The result was ISO 31000, published in November 2009. The same day, Standards Australia adopted the international standard in place of its own by releasing Australian/New Zealand Standard Risk Management Principles and Guidelines AS/NZS ISO 31000: 2009. Similarly, in Canada ISO 31000 has been adopted as a national standard through the Canadian Standards Authority. In March 2010, the British Standards Institute also integrated the international standard into its own portfolio, as BS ISO 31000. In the past, some commentators have suggested that the slow adoption of formalized risk management systems can be blamed, in part, upon the array of system choices open to organizations, with North American companies adopting COSO, the Canadians referencing CoCO, and Europeans and Australians using their own local standards. ISO 31000 is not only internationally accepted, but is also described as useful for all organizations, regardless of type and size. It is the claimed universal applicability of ISO 31000 which makes it highly significant and also potentially extremely influential.

ISO 31000 clearly builds on the elements contained within the original 1995 AS/NSZ 4360, but at the same time it reflects the evolution in thinking in risk management that has occurred in the intervening years. In particular, the new standard emphasizes the need for embedding the risk management framework into an organization. Whilst ISO 31000 simply uses the term risk management framework, within the UK, the Institute of Risk Management's (IRM) has published guidelines which explicitly describe the framework as one of ERM, in line with the language used in COSO 2004. In so doing, the IRM suggest that it is possible to put in place a risk management system which is compatible with both COSO (2004) and ISO 31000 (2009). It is therefore important to recognize that COSO 2004 was a stepping stone in the development of thinking about risk management standards, and hence an important influence upon today's ISO 31000.

COSO 2004 – Enterprise Risk Management: Integrated Framework

In Chapter 2 the section on the phases of regulatory change included discussion of the historic events which led to the establishment of the first COSO framework in 1992 and its subsequent redrafting in 2004. Most importantly, it was noted that the 1992 version positioned risk assessment as a sub-element of a broader internal control framework aimed at providing assurance to stakeholders. In contrast, the 2004 version reversed the relative importance of risk management and internal control by renaming risk management as 'enterprise risk management', and defining it as a term 'that incorporates the internal control framework within it' (COSO 2004, foreword, p. v).

The idea of ERM as the overarching framework for internal control implies that 'risk is embodied within the corporate strategy of an enterprise' (Dickinson, 2001, p. 364). As a result, when corporate objectives are aligned with those of shareholders, then ERM also provides a framework for managing shareholder value. The link between risk management and shareholder value is well supported in the practitioner literature; see, for example, the booklet published by the International Federation of Accountants' (IFAC) Management Accounting Committee and CIMA in 2002 entitled *Managing Risk to Enhance Shareholder Value*, which contains some nice examples of risk management practice in a range of public and private sector organizations. This literature reiterates, albeit in a different way, the idea that reputation is a valuable asset.

COSO 2004 defines ERM as follows:

> a process, effected by an entity's board of directors, management and other personnel, applied in strategy setting and across the enterprise, designed to identify potential events that may affect the entity, and manage risk to be within its risk appetite, to provide reasonable assurance regarding the achievement of entity objectives.

A number of key elements are contained within this definition.

- ERM is embodied within the organizational strategy.
- ERM takes an enterprise wide view of risks.
- Staff at every level of the organization are involved in ERM.
- Identification of risks which may threaten the achievement of objectives is central to ERM.
- Risks are managed within the context of a specified risk appetite.

COSO 2004 also defines four categories of organizational objectives:

- *Strategic:* the high level goals, e.g. market share.
- *Operations:* ensuring efficient use of physical and human resources.
- *Reporting:* reliability in reporting to stakeholders.
- *Compliance:* with applicable laws and regulations.

If an ERM system is designed with all four overlapping objectives in mind, then it creates a framework that is about more than just compliance. Sadly, the way that COSO 2004 has been widely used as the benchmark for evaluation of compliance by North American companies with Sarbanes Oxley, has resulted in much stronger emphasis being placed on the compliance objective, over and above the other three. The result has been a distortion of the underlying philosophy of ERM.

Within COSO, the broadly based management of risks within ERM is achieved through the establishment of eight components which in combination make up a control framework (Box 3.1). The COSO framework uses what is termed the COSO cube (Figure 3.2), to create a matrix which links the three dimensions of the internal control system: the organizational objectives, the organization structure and the components of the internal control system.

Box 3.1 Components of Enterprise Risk Management

- *Internal Environment.* The culture of the organization, its ethical stance, risk appetite and internal attitude to risk management.
- *Objective setting.* Organizational objectives must be clearly specified, linked to strategies and reflect the overall risk appetite.
- *Event identification.* Both risks and opportunities which might affect the achievement of objectives are identified.
- *Risk Assessment.* Risks are assessed taking into account a combination of both their likelihood and impact.
- *Risk response.* In line with the risk appetite, decisions are taken on whether to accept, avoid, reduce or share the risks.
- *Activities.* Policies and procedures are laid down to ensure that risks management procedures are implemented.
- *Information and communication.* Information is collected and communicated throughout the organization about the risks and the associated lines of responsibility for their management.
- *Monitoring.* The ERM framework is continually monitored and revised as necessary across the whole organization.

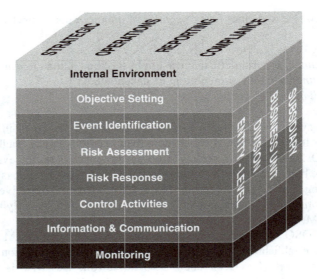

Figure 3.2 The COSO cube

Source: Coso, *Enterprise Risk Management* (2004) used by permission

The COSO cube neatly illustrates the idea that ERM straddles the entire organization by applying a common framework for the control of risks. The backbone of any risk management system is represented by the systems used to facilitate the IDENTIFICATION, and ASSESSMENT of risks, together with a decision on the RISK RESPONSE, systems of risk REPORTING and ongoing MONITORING. All of these steps take into account the organizational context and its specific set of objectives. These core components can also be found within ISO 31000 (2009) (and its predecessors). In fact ISO 31000 mirrors COSO 2004 very closely, as is shown below, although the term 'components' is used differently in the two standards.

Components of ISO 31000

ISO 31000 is made up of three linked components:

- Risk management principles, similar to the key elements of the ERM definition in COSO.
- Risk management framework.
- Risk management process, similar to the ERM components in COSO.

The interaction between the three components is shown in Figure 3.3. The figure shows that the principles are used as an input to the creation of a risk management framework, which is put into practice via the establishment of the risk management process. As the diagram indicates, neither the framework or process are static as monitoring and continual review results in process changes which in turn refine the framework as lessons are learnt and changes to systems are implemented. The idea is that the structures and mechanisms used to manage risks are continually evolving in response to organizational change.

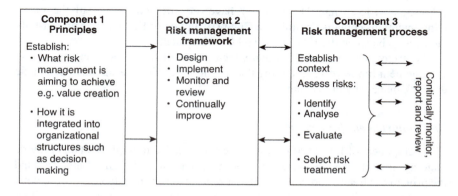

Figure 3.3 Linking the three components of ISO 31000

Source: Based on ISO 31000

The content of the main standard is complemented by ISO Guide 73: 2009, *Risk Management: Terminology*, which provides a collection of terms and definitions relating to the management of risk and ISO/IEC 31010: 2009, *Risk Management: Risk Assessment Techniques*, which provides guidance on selection and application of systematic techniques for risk assessment. This guidance on implementation was not present in the AS/NSZ 4360 (1995) standard.

Risk management principles

The principles within ISO 31000 are intended to ensure that organizations seek to improve their performance by embedding risk management within their own specific organizational context. The eleven principles state that risk management should:

(a) Create and protect value.
(b) Be an integral part of all organizational processes.
(c) Be part of decision-making.
(d) Address uncertainty explicitly.
(e) Be systematic, structured and timely.
(f) Be based on the best available information.
(g) Be tailored to the needs of the organization.
(h) Take into account human and cultural factors.
(i) Promote transparency and inclusiveness.
(j) Be dynamic, iterative and responsive to change.
(k) Facilitate continual improvement to the organization.

These principles are not formulaic and also suggest that investment in risk management systems should be proportional to organizational needs. In this way the standard can be adapted to suit different types and scales of organization. At the same time the principles reiterate the case for integrating risk awareness into the culture of the organization – so that it is systematic, incorporated into decision-making and yet responsive to change. The principles have very strong overlaps with the underlying intentions contained within the COSO definition of ERM and again illustrate the overlap between the ISO 31000 and COSO systems.

The principles form a basis upon which an organization can construct a risk management framework, and imply that a central decision has already been made that risk management is beneficial.

Risk management framework

This component of ISO 31000 outlines the steps needed to implement and provide ongoing support for a risk management system. The initial design is framed around the principles already laid down, so that it reflects the organizational context, what they want to achieve from risk management and how it is to be embedded within the organization, as indicated in Figure 3.2. Implementation of the framework is rapidly followed by implementation of the process (component 3) and both are the subject of continual internal reporting and monitoring so that both processes and the framework can be continually improved and refined.

Risk management process

The process represents the real 'meat' of the risk management system and contains the core elements that also appear in the COSO cube, as summarized earlier. The process incorporates the following elements:

- Establish context.
- Assess risks:
  - a.)   Analyse.
  - b.)   Evaluate.
- Select risk treatment.
- Communicate and consult.
- Monitor and review.

It is not difficult to see the strong similarities between COSO and ISO 31000.

The stepped process of assessment, identification, analysis and treatment of risks was first laid down in the original 1995 version of AS/NSZ 4360, and the version in ISO 31000 is simply an extended form of that idea, which now embraces risks across the full breadth of an organization. In other words it has evolved over time into an enterprise risk management process. At the end of the day, however, it is the way in which the process is implemented that can make or break a risk management system. Some discussion of each of the elements of the process is therefore important.

Establish context

The culture of the organization and the attitude to risk that it engenders is very important as it creates the context within which risks will be managed. If staff are encouraged to be 'risk aware' and take responsibility for the control of risks then the ERM system will be very different from one in an organization where risk taking is encouraged as a way of boosting short term profits. The general attitude to risk within an organization, and its risk appetite will commonly reflect the views of the Board of Directors and other senior managers, and this may be formalized in the production of documented guidance and rules on risk taking. The case studies in Chapters 4–7 illustrate very different attitudes to risk within the different organizations, and serve to emphasize the significance of context within the risk management process.

Assess risks

Risk assessment involves three sub-elements of identification, analysis and evaluation, which help a manager to decide how to respond to a specific risk, given the organization's risk appetite. Risk identification requires the specification of the many threats and opportunities that may impact upon company objectives and construction of a categorization system, as discussed in the first part of this chapter. Risk identification is required at all levels of the organization – from strategy level, through to day-to-day operational activities and special projects, and may be undertaken using either a top-down or bottom-up approach. Whichever method is adopted, it is helpful to understand that risk identification is the responsibility of operating staff and not specialized risk management staff. The managers know the issues facing their business and are therefore best equipped to be able to identify the related risks. It is not uncommon, however, for risk management staff to be involved in training managers on identification techniques. A range of techniques can be used for risk assessment including:

- Questionnaires and checklists.
- Interviews and focus groups.
- Workshops and brainstorming.
- Flow charts and dependency analysis.
- Inspection and audits.
- SWOT (strengths, weaknesses, opportunities and threats) analysis.
- PESTLE (political, economic, social, technological, legal and economic) analysis.

Once identified, the risks need to be both categorized and recorded, with decisions being made about the nature and level of detail to be held on each risk. Risk registers, sometimes called risk logs, will commonly be maintained for each business area and special project, as well as at top level for the overall organization. The key risk register, maintained at the top level, will record only those risks seen as posing a significant threat to the overall organization, and these risks will be regularly discussed at Board of Director meetings, and ideally managed or 'owned' by a senior executive. The case studies in this book include examples of risk registers. A typical register, such as that illustrated in Figure 3.4, will include a brief description of the risk, the manager/person held responsible for it, the risk assessment, the decision on risk treatment and the residual risk remaining after treatment. Frequency of monitoring, or the date of the next review may also be included.

Risk analysis and evaluation involve consideration of both the likelihood and impact of the risk and the allocation of a risk rating or score. Impact and likelihood are frequently measured using either 3×3 or 5×5 matrices, which rank on a scale of low to very high, as shown in Figure 3.5. Key risks will be numbered and marked on the squares in the matrix. The top right hand side of the matrix, indicates risks which need to be actively managed because they have both a high likelihood of occurrence as well as high impact. Moving towards the bottom left of the matrix represents a lower risk management priority. The levels of risk from very high (top right) to low (bottom left), are usually represented as deep red, red, amber and green (shown in Figure 3.5 as shades of grey), giving a

Risk management

Risk identified	Risk owner	Risk analysis			Risk management strategy			Action plan		Risk mitigation status
		Impact	Likelihood	Risk score	Mitigation/Controls	Effectiveness	Assurance	Further action required	Person responsible/Date	
Risk number Risk description Risk detail Risk causes Risk effects										①
										②
										③

Figure 3.4 Risk register template. The shaded risk mitigation column will actually be coloured red, amber or green to indicate the risk evaluation, and the risk register will include definitions of each category, e.g. red: residual risk level is unacceptable; amber: residual risk level not unacceptable but at a level requiring further mitigation; green: tolerable residual risk level.

Note: As this Figure is in black and white 1. red, 2. amber, and 3. green.

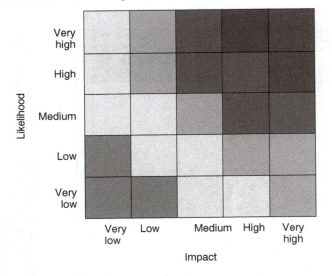

Figure 3.5 Likelihood: consequences matrix

clear visual profile of risk from high priority (deep red) to acceptable (green). The number of squares on the grid which are coloured red, amber or green will reflect the organisation, or business unit's appetite for risk. Figure 3.5 shows a low level of risk tolerance, as only three out of twenty-five squares indicate acceptable levels of risk.

Select risk treatment

Selection of a *risk treatment* follows naturally on from the evaluation process. In ISO 31000 risk treatment refers to the activity of selecting and implementing appropriate control measures to modify the risk. As such, whilst risk control or mitigation are central to risk treatment, the terms also includes risk avoidance, risk transfer and risk financing.

From the evaluation process, any risks labelled as amber or red require a mitigating response and so alternative options will be evaluated on the basis of their cost and expected impact on both the likelihood and impact of the selected risk. The control needs to be both effective in reducing the risks, but also efficient in terms of its cost. The four alternative types of treatment or responses to risk are:

- *Risk acceptance:* do nothing.
- *Risk reduction:* this may be aimed at either reducing the likelihood of occurrence e.g. via regular maintenance of equipment to prevent breakdowns; or it could aim to reduce the impact of a risk occurring e.g. through disaster recovery plans; provision of back-up facilities, etc.

- *Risk transfer:* for example through the purchase of a form of risk financing such as insurance.
- *Risk avoidance:* by eliminating the activities which create a given risk.

Attitudes to both evaluation and treatment may change over time as an organization's risk appetite alters. For example, the listed Malaysian company K-one Technology saw its profits fall from RM6.05 million in 2008 to just RM1.27 million in 2009 as a result of foreign exchange losses. In response, a decision was taken to hedge foreign exchange risks by using natural (internal) hedging, and to date the policy seems to be paying off as profits are once again rising.

Communicate and consult, and monitor and review

Communication, consultation, monitoring and review are all types of feedback controls which help to ensure the ongoing effectiveness of a risk management system. In feeding back information on risk management, the aim is to communicate how well risks are being managed, how and if controls are working and where they are not, and suggest ways in which the whole process can be improved. Communication of risk information should be both internal, for control purposes, but also external, for reasons of accountability. Keeping stakeholders informed about the risks faced and the actions being taken to manage them will provide reassurance. In efficient markets, good risk disclosures might also be expected to reduce the cost of capital for those organizations that demonstrate effective risk management. There is a growing academic literature on the topic of risk reporting, an analysis of which is outside the scope of this book (see end of chapter references for some examples). To date, however, the consensus view from researchers seems to be that much of the information on risk that is included in company annual reports is boilerplate in nature and not particularly useful (see, for example, Woods *et al.*, 2009).

Internal communication and monitoring will be two directional. Managers will be reporting upwards about how risks are being managed, and the internal audit function will similarly be reporting back on the effectiveness of existing controls. This feedback should be working to drive both the frequency and type of control monitoring that is being undertaken and also the potential redesign of existing systems. The internal audit function plays a key role in the monitoring process, and so it is important that they retain independent judgement. Those who design internal controls should not also be responsible for their evaluation, and so managing the relationship between internal audit and risk management staff is an essential part of maintaining an effective risk management system.

Summary

Risk management standards such as COSO and ISO 31000 provide a framework for the creation of what is sometimes termed the risk architecture of an organization. The term architecture refers to the structures used for recording,

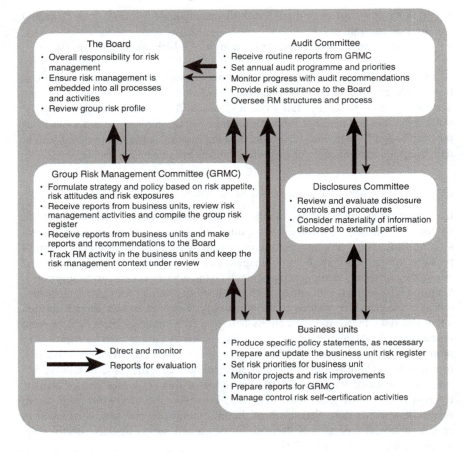

The Board
- Overall responsibility for risk management
- Ensure risk management is embedded into all processes and activities
- Review group risk profile

Audit Committee
- Receive routine reports from GRMC
- Set annual audit programme and priorities
- Monitor progress with audit recommendations
- Provide risk assurance to the Board
- Oversee RM structures and process

Group Risk Management Committee (GRMC)
- Formulate strategy and policy based on risk appetite, risk attitudes and risk exposures
- Receive reports from business units, review risk management activities and compile the group risk register
- Receive reports from business units and make reports and recommendations to the Board
- Track RM activity in the business units and keep the risk management context under review

Disclosures Committee
- Review and evaluate disclosure controls and procedures
- Consider materiality of information disclosed to external parties

Direct and monitor
Reports for evaluation

Business units
- Produce specific policy statements, as necessary
- Prepare and update the business unit risk register
- Set risk priorities for business unit
- Monitor projects and risk improvements
- Prepare reports for GRMC
- Manage control risk self-certification activities

Figure 3.6 Risk architecture of a large PLC

Source: Airmic, Alarm and IRM, *A Structured Approach to Enterprise Risk Management and the Requirements of ISO 31000* (2010, p. 12)

managing, reporting and monitoring risks, and the example that follows is taken from the current Airmic/Alarm/IRM guidance on implementing ERM and ISO 31000 (2010).

The precise design of the architecture will vary across organizations because it will be modified to reflect differences in levels of organizational complexity. As indicated at the start of this section, the aim of the risk standards is not to be prescriptive but to offer guidance on how risks can be managed in any size and type of organization, and so not all organizations will have, for example, a group risk management committee, or a disclosures committee as shown in Figure 3.6. Nonetheless, in some shape or form, all organizations seeking to implement ERM will have systems for the identification, assessment, and treatment of risks together with support for monitoring and review of the risk controls.

ERM in practice

The spirit underpinning the risk management standards discussed above may be laudable but it remains an open question as to the extent to which ERM is actually being effectively put into practice. From a theoretical and conceptual perspective it is difficult to challenge the suggestion that an organization needs to adopt a systematic and holistic approach to the management of its risks, as encapsulated within the idea of ERM. Putting such a vision into practice, however, seems to be proving extremely challenging. Reporting on the results of an in depth interview survey of corporate treasurers across Europe, the Association of Corporate Treasurers noted that whilst most respondents had some sort of ERM system in place, many were compliance led, and driven by regulations and governance codes (ACT, 2006). As a result, risks tended to be addressed individually, and were not incorporated into decision-making in the manner intended under ERM.

Even the Institute of Internal Auditors acknowledges that if you ask 100 people for a definition of ERM you will get at least 100 different answers, ranging from the highly technical, quantitatively driven models to those which are less formalized and decentralized. The financial crisis has led many to the view that highly quantitative systems will tend to fail simply because they miss certain types of risk, but the crisis has been limited in the lessons it has offered up regarding exactly what types of ERM system might succeed. In fact, it is most likely the case that the ERM model which works for firm X will not be the same as the one which works for firm Y, simply because the context is different. Effective risk management comes back to understanding what an organization is trying to achieve and constructing controls which reflect the desired risk appetite. Changes in any or all of the size of organization, its field of operation, or its objectives are likely to impact upon the risk appetite and require modifications to the risk management system. The case studies which follow shed some light on this idea and demonstrate the importance of good internal and external communication as a way of enhancing the effectiveness of risk management.

Who is responsible for risk management?

Whilst people from right across an organization will hold some individual responsibility for risk management, certain parties take on very specific responsibilities and it is important that these are documented and clearly communicated.

Overall responsibility for risk management rests at the top of an organization, with the Board of Directors or their equivalent. Board members determine the objectives and strategies as well as the level of risk that the organization will tolerate, and they must also be satisfied that the controls over risks are effective in maintaining risk exposures within the bounds of the risk appetite. Under the governance regulations, the Board of Directors are responsible for the annual review of internal controls and decisions on appropriate responses.

In larger organizations, the Board of Directors is commonly supported in its responsibilities for risk management by an Audit Committee. Committee members liaise with both internal and external audit staff and feed back their findings to the executive management. As such the Audit Committee is often seen as the key party responsible for risk management, particularly in view of their role in overseeing the work of internal audit, which tests the effectiveness of internal controls. The case studies show that Audit Committees are no longer confined to the private sector, as New Public Management has encouraged their introduction across the public sector.

Moving beyond the Board of Directors and Audit Committee and further down into an organization, the lines of responsibility for risk management are laid down in the risk architecture, such as that illustrated in Figure 3.6. As already indicated, however, the architectural design is not prescribed. Consequently, the question of exactly who takes responsibility for what in terms of risk management, and the lines used for internal reporting can be seen to vary widely in practice. Unfortunately, it is also the case that there is an absence of academic research into alternative models of risk management and their relative merits. The practitioner literature includes a lot of recommendations on how to establish a risk management system but the evidence underpinning the recommendations seems almost non-existent. Similarly, individual case studies which document practice in specific organizations do not provide critical and comparative analysis of alternative approaches. An important objective of this book is to use the case studies as a tool to give readers the opportunity to compare different risk management systems, and in Chapter 8 we look at the lessons that can be drawn from such a comparison. For now, however, we return to the question of 'who is responsible for risk management?'

Given the wide range of risks that may be faced by an organization, a number of different professional parties may seek claim to being responsible for risk management to a greater or lesser degree. Such parties, and the reasons for their claim to expertise, include:

- *Insurance professionals*, as the people responsible for the original function out of which risk management originally emerged.
- *Accountants*, including both management accountants who are experts in the design and maintenance of internal control systems and chartered accountants, whose experience of auditing can be applied to the monitoring and review of risk controls.
- *Internal auditors* have for a long time been seeking to define themselves in terms of a distinctive profession which adds value through the improvement of risk management, control and governance processes.
- *Actuaries* whose are experts in the pricing of risk and specifically pension risk (which is rapidly growing in significance).
- *Financial economists* as the designers of both financial products and quantitative models that can be used in risk management.

- *Corporate treasurers*, who have long standing expertise in managing foreign exchange and interest rate risks, as well as balance sheet structuring.

In the light of so many claims to expertise the scope for different answers to the question 'Who is responsible for risk management?' are almost infinite and it is impossible to prescribe a single ideal approach. At the same time, it is clear that the risk function is becoming increasingly professionalized, particularly with the emergence of the Chief Risk Officer (CRO) role, which is now common in North America, although less so in the UK. Hutter and Power (2005) cite James Lam of GE Capital as being the first person to be appointed (in 1993) to the post of CRO. The creation of this role is linked to the broadening of the concept of risk management away from simply insurance or financial risk and into enterprise risk management. At the same time, it reflects a shift in thinking about risk that takes it out of the back office and onto centre stage in relation to strategy.

One justification for the CRO role is the need for a co-ordinator who has some expertise in risk management. No single individual could keep track of all of the risks in the multiple divisions of even a small listed company; in the public sector, where risks are perhaps even more diverse and potentially catastrophic, the problems are exacerbated further. The CRO can be the expert in terms of the governance regulations and risk management standards, whilst leaving the detail of how to manage particular categories of risk to the functional experts. Actuaries manage the pension risk; treasurers look after the financial risk and so on.

But maybe the job of the CRO goes beyond that of a co-ordinator and extends into actively monitoring risks and controls and alerting senior management to problems? A case study of the introduction of ERM into a Canadian electric utility company, Hydro One (Aabo *et al.*, 2005) argues that the company's appointment of a CRO and subsequent refinements to its risk management system greatly strengthened the company, and also improved its credit rating. Whether or not the CRO really has influence over risk management policies, and particularly with senior staff is very dependent upon their position within the organizational hierarchy. Below Board of Director level, a CRO has little or no power if the Board choose not to listen.

Some organizations hold the view that appointing a CRO is not appropriate. For example, Tesco's response to the Financial Reporting Council's review of the UK's Combined Code in 2009 argues that making companies create a separate risk committee (as in Figure 3.6) or appoint a CRO 'may hinder a company's ability to structure their risk management approach according to their business model and the environment within which they operate' (Tesco, 2009).

At the root of ERM is the idea that risk management is embedded right across an organization, and consequently is the responsibility of everyone. Specialist experts have their place, but they need support from operational staff. This takes us back to the nub of the problem with risk management. Standards and regulations have only limited usefulness because ultimately, as already noted, compliance with a standard does not necessarily result in an effective risk management system. Effectiveness comes from ensuring that risk management is integral to the activities of the company. The case studies that follow indicate wide varia-tions in the level of integration across the different organizations.

Conclusion

This chapter has demonstrated the complexities of installing a risk management system in three different ways. First, by highlighting the vast array of risks faced by today's organizations; second, by demonstrating that risk categorization and the adoption of risk management standards provide a framework for risk manage-ment that has some (but limited) value and lastly by arguing that responsibility for risk management permeates an organization. The Board of Directors carry ultimate responsibility for the internal control and governance system and also establishing the organization's risk appetite, but no risk architecture, even one incorporating a CRO or risk committee can overcome the need to embed the control of risk into the day-to-day business of the organization. Therein lies the challenge and the following four chapters illustrate how different major organizations have responded to that challenge in a variety of ways.

References

Aabo, T., Fraser, J. and Simkins, B. (2005) 'The rise and evolution of the chief risk officer: enterprise risk management at Hydro One', *Journal of Applied Corporate Finance*, Vol. 17, No. 3, pp. 62–75.

ACT (with Mercer Oliver Wyman) (2006) *The Role of the Treasurer in Enterprise Risk Management*, ACT, London.

Airmic, ALARM and IRM (2010) *A Structured Approach to Enterprise Risk Management and the Requirements of ISO 31000*, available for download free of charge from the web sites of each of these organizations.

Committee of Sponsoring Organizations of the Treadway Commission (COSO) (1992) *Internal Control – Integrated Framework*, American Institute of Certified Public Accountants, Jersey City, NJ.

Committee of Sponsoring Organisations of the Treadway Commission (COSO) (2004) *Enterprise Risk Management*, AICPA, New York.

Dickinson, G. (2001) 'Enterprise risk management: its origins and conceptual foundation', *Geneva Papers on Risk and Insurance*, Vol. 36, No. 3 (July), pp. 360–6.

Economist Intelligence Unit (2005) *Reputation: Risk of Risks*, EIU, London.

Hutter, B. and Power, M. (eds) (2005) *Organizational Encounters with Risk*, Cambridge University Press, Cambridge.

Leitch, M. (2010) ISO Guide 73 (2009) Risk Management: Vocabulary, International Organization for Standardization (ISO), Geneva.

Leitch, M. (2010) ISO 31000:2009 – The New International Standard on Risk Management. *Risk Analysis*, 30:887–892.

Peters, T. (1989) 'Tomorrow's companies', *The Economist*, 4 March, pp. 27–30.

Tesco (2009) Response to the Corporate Governance Unit of the FRC, October, http://www.frc.org.uk/documents/pagemanager/frc/Responses_to_July_consultation/Tesco.pdf

Woods, M., Humphrey, C. and Dowd, K. (2009) 'Market risk reporting by the world's top banks: evidence on the diversity of reporting practice and the implications for international accounting harmonisation', *Revista de Contabilidad – Spanish Accounting Review*, Vol. 11, No. 2, pp. 9–42.

Useful web links

- http://www.garp.org/ is the web site of the US-based Global Association of Risk Professionals, and is a useful illustration of how this new profession has developed and created its own certification programmes and qualification system.
- The websites of the Big Four accounting firms all have risk consultancy sections, which contain useful publications on risk-related issues and information on the type of risk advisory services they provide: Price Waterhouse Coopers, www.pwc.com; KPMG, http://rd.kpmg.co.uk/14502.htm; Deloitte, www.deloitte.com; Ernst & Young, www.ey.com

Discussion questions

1   Analyse your own position – either as a student or as an employee – specify your medium term objectives, and list all of the risks that may threaten your ability to achieve those objectives. Group the risks into categories, identify the key risks and try and construct a likelihood consequences matrix for the key risks. What have you learnt from this exercise?
2   Look at the latest annual reports of *two* of the FTSE 100 companies and/or *two* public sector organizations such as government departments or local councils. What do they tell you about their exposure to risk, the quality of internal controls and the effectiveness of the risk management system? To what extent should an organization report about risk management to its stakeholders?

Part II

Risk management in practice

The private sector

4 Case study

Tesco PLC

Company profile

History

Tesco PLC, now one of the largest retailers in the world, is also one of the most admired. In the year in which the interviews for this case study were conducted, Tesco was voted the fifth most respected retailer in the world, and the group's chief executive, Sir Terry Leahy, was ranked 34th amongst the world's most respected corporate leaders.[1]

Tesco was founded in 1924 by Jack Cohen, who started out as an East End market trader. After visiting the United States, Cohen decided to introduce the self-service supermarket approach to food retailing, and the first Tesco branch in this style was opened in 1947. Since then the company has gone through a series of stages of development, to bring it to its current status as a global company.

The early 1970s saw Tesco rebrand itself as an 'aspirational' mass retailer rather than a discounter, and this period also saw a deal between Tesco and Esso which by 1991 made them the country's largest independent petrol retailer. The 1980s were a decade during which Tesco rationalized and reformatted its distribution systems, launched its first 'out-of-town' shopping centres, and began introducing its own product lines to compete against traditionally branded products.

By the start of the 1990s Tesco had 371 stores in England, Scotland and Wales, and its expansion during the next few years was characterized by the introduction of the Tesco Metro format of mid-size stores (around 1,100 m^2) and substantial investment in new outlets. By 1995 they were ranked the number one food retailer in the UK, and the same year they became the first UK retailer to introduce a loyalty card, which has proved a valuable source of information on customer spending patterns as well as a useful marketing tool.

The 1990s also marked the start of Tesco's development as an international retailer, with its investments in acquisitions in France, Poland, Slovakia and the Czech Republic. Heavy investment in Eastern Europe paid off relatively quickly, and it was followed by further international expansion into South East Asia via acquisitions and joint ventures in South Korea, Thailand, Malaysia, Taiwan, Japan and China. As a result, by early 2004 the retail selling space outside the UK closely followed that of the home market, although sales and profit per square metre remained lower. In the financial year ending February 2009, the total overseas floor area was 80 per cent greater than that of the UK.

In Tesco's core UK market continued sales growth has been aided by extending into the convenience store sector.[2] This process began in 2002 with the acquisition of the 1,200 outlets of T & S Stores. Some of the smallest stores were sold on, and others converted into Tesco Express local convenience stores and One Stop, which are the smallest shops operated by the company, and the only ones not to include the Tesco name.

Not content with expanding its business in traditional retailing, Tesco has also established a strong presence in the e-commerce market place. Tesco.com was launched in 2000, and the grocery home shopping service has since developed into the largest of its kind in the world. The development helped to reinforce the company's strength in its core market, so that in 2009 it held a 22 per cent and 8.8 per cent share in the UK's grocery and non-food markets.

In 2008, in the wake of the banking crisis, Tesco took full ownership of Tesco Personal Finance, the joint venture business it started with the Royal Bank of Scotland in 1997. Tesco has recently proclaimed its commitment to extending its involvement in the financial services arena and this issue is discussed in some depth in the subsequent case study.

Main competitors

Asda, J. Sainsbury, Wm Morrison.

Stock market listing(s)

London. (ADRs also available through Deutsche Bank Trust Company Americas.)

Store formats

- *Tesco Extra.* Large, out-of-town hypermarkets (some exceptions are in town).
- *Tesco Superstore.* Standard large supermarkets, accounting for the bulk of the company's UK floorspace. Average size 2,900 m^2.
- *Tesco Metro.* Small supermarkets in city centres or town/village high streets. Average size 1,100 m^2.
- *Tesco Express.* Local convenience stores, including petrol forecourt outlets. Average size 190 m^2.
- *One Stop.* The smallest shops, commonly with late opening hours. Average size 125 m^2.

Since 2005 Tesco have also opened a number of non-food outlets under the name of Tesco Homeplus, and in late 2007 they purchased a chain of 21 garden centres in Scotland.

Key dates

1932 Tesco Stores Ltd founded
1947 First Tesco self-service store opened, in St Albans
1983 Name changed to Tesco PLC
1985 Hundredth superstore opened in England
1992 Tesco Metro format introduced
1994 First move into Central Europe (Hungary)
1994 First Tesco Express petrol station opened
1997 Tesco Personal Finance established in a joint venture with Royal Bank of Scotland
1997 Terry Leahy appointed Chief Executive
1998 First move into South East Asia through purchase of a stake in the Lotus chain of convenience stores
2000 Internet retail business launched: Tesco.com
2004 Purchase of a share in a Chinese-owned hypermarket chain
2007 First Fresh and Easy store opened, in California
2008 First wholly owned Tesco store opened in Guangzhou, China
2008 Tesco buys out RBS's share of Tesco Personal Finance for £950 million to become sole owner of the financial services company
2009 Underlying pre-tax profits of £3.13 billion reported for year ending February 2009

The summary above of the historical development of Tesco PLC, with Tables 4.1 and 4.2, indicates an organization that is continually evolving its

Table 4.1 Geographic spread of operations

	Year ending February			
	2004	*2009*	*2004*	*2009*
Region	*No. of stores*		*Retail space (m² million)*	
United Kingdom	1,878	2,282[a]	2.39	2.91
Rest of Europe: Irish Republic, Czech Republic, Hungary, Poland, Slovakia, Turkey	261	863	1.09	
Asia: Malaysia, South Korea, Taiwan, Thailand, Japan, South Korea, India	179	1,047	0.95	5.11
United States	0	115	0	0.2[b]
Total non-UK	440	2,025	2.22	5.31
Total	2,318	4,307[a]		8.22

Notes: [a]Excludes 28 Dobbies stores. [b]Calculated from global total less known regional statistics.

Table 4.2 Key statistics

Statistic	Year ending February			
	1995	*1999*	*2004ᵃ*	*2009*
Turnover excluding VAT (£ million):				
• UK	9,655	15,835	24,760	38,191
• Rest of Europe	4,616	1,167	3,385	8,862
• Asia (excluding China)	Nil	156ᵇ	2,669	7,068ᶜ
• China	Nil	Nil		702
• Total	10,101	17,158	30,184	47,298
Group operating margin (%)	6.1	5.6	5.9	5.9
Profit before taxation (£ million)	551	842	1,600	2,954
Earnings per share (£0.01)	6.90	9.59	16.45	28.92
Full time equivalent employees (No.)	68,552	108,284	152,408	468,508
Total sales area (ft² 000)	12,641	15,975	45,402	88,451

Notes: ᵃ Fifty-three weeks. ᵇ Thailand only. ᶜ Includes China in 2009.

strategies over time in order to ensure sustained growth. At the same time, its relatively consistent operating margins and growth of earnings per share suggest that these evolving strategies pose limited risks to shareholders.

The case study which follows draws upon material contained in the annual reports of Tesco PLC and information collected from extended interviews with senior members of staff in the internal audit division of the company. The aim of the study is to provide some insights into the structures used for risk management within Tesco PLC, and the tools that are used by the company to manage the risks associated with its position as a major global retailer.

Sources of data reported in the case study

The material used in the case study is drawn from a number of different sources, but primarily upon internal documentation from the company and interview transcripts. In preparation for the interviews, publicly available information on the risk management system and practices was reviewed, and this has constantly been reviewed in the period since the interviews, to ensure that all information is fully up to date as of mid-2009.

Risk management: an overview

Any attempts to summarize the risk management system within an organization that is of the scale of Tesco will inevitably fail to cover many issues, and so focusing on the features that are most striking to an outside observer provides a useful starting point for understanding the organization's approach to risk management.

CIMA's Official Terminology (CIMA, 2005, p. 20) defines performance measurement as: 'the process of assessing the proficiency with which a reporting entity succeeds ... in achieving its objectives'. The same terminology (CIMA, 2005, p. 53) defines risk management as the 'process of understanding and managing the risks that the entity is inevitably subject to in attempting to achieve its corporate objectives'.

It would therefore seem that it is difficult, if not impossible, to talk about risk management without simultaneously talking about performance management – the two go hand in hand. This integration of risk and performance thinking is straightforward in theory but not so easy to implement in practice, but it forms the blueprint for Tesco's approach to risk management. In order to understand how this is implemented it is helpful to map out the way in which objectives are operationalized within a business.

Traditional theory argues that it is the role of senior management to translate objectives into detailed strategies, which are influenced by both external and internal factors. An organization's external environment, in terms of the regulatory regimes, economic conditions, industry structure and levels of competition may restrict strategic choices. Additionally, it is widely acknowledged (see for example Band and Scanlon, 1995) that good 'strategic fit' (Waterman, 1986) is fundamental to organizational success, where the term 'fit' refers to the need for strategies to reflect internal characteristics of the business. These include human resources, culture, systems and structures.

Risk management is one of the structures within this framework, and so it is important for it to also reflect and fit in with the factors seen to influence strategies, both internally and externally. Tesco provides a good illustration of how corporate strategies, structures, control systems, people and culture interact to create an organization with specific individual characteristics. The nature and strength of the interactions can be expected to vary across organizations, with the result that risk management systems may vary widely even across apparently similar organizations. This characteristic is clearly demonstrated across the series of case studies of which this forms a part.

Risk management within Tesco: internal influences

The risk management system reflects and responds to the following powerful internal influences:

- The influence of the CEO, Sir Terry Leahy.
- The corporate culture and resulting corporate control systems.
- The nature of the business and particularly its overall simplicity – in essence it is a distribution business.
- Organizational structure, particularly the limited number of managerial levels within its relatively 'flat' structure.

Each of these influences is now discussed in some depth:

Sir Terry Leahy

The first page of the 2009 Annual Report expounds the organizational philosophy in its declaration that 'Tesco is about creating value for customers to earn their lifetime loyalty'. This is reiterated a few pages later (p. 8) in the statement that 'At the core of Tesco's business model is a focus on trying to improve what we do for customers'.

This philosophy directly reflects the viewpoint of the CEO, Sir Terry Leahy, who is totally customer focused. His argument is that keeping customers happy is fundamental to success and this perspective is embedded in all staff from day one. Gaining staff support for the business philosophy is not only good for customers, however, but also for the overall organization. The average longevity of people within the Tesco management team is around 14 years, and maintaining a global staff retention rate in excess of 80 per cent[3] is one of the company's key performance indicators. Consequently, recruitment and training costs are reduced, resulting in higher returns to shareholders.

The interviews and supplementary informal research suggest that knowledge of Leahy's priorities permeates the full length of the organizational hierarchy. Checkout and shelf filling staff within stores know that the sound bites that are so familiar to Tesco customers such as 'every little helps' should be reflected in their own patterns of behaviour. Company wide, it seems to be accepted that if the business is performing well in the eyes of the customer, then it will also be performing well for other stakeholders. As one interviewee phrased it: 'the biggest barometer we've got is our customers ... how can we earn their lifetime loyalty?'

In practical terms, this results in a strong internal focus within the business. It was suggested that if you accept that 'Terry's philosophy is very clear. If you look at the customer and you are doing what the customer wants, you don't have to spend your energies worrying about competitors'. Not everyone would necessarily agree with such a perspective, but it has the advantage of providing a clear and simple message by which to guide staff thinking and behaviour. Furthermore, Leahy's emphasis on customer needs taking priority over worrying about the competition exactly matches the thinking of Kenichi Ohmae, a former partner in McKinsey & Co. and a man widely described as 'Mr Strategy'. Ohmae takes the view that 'before you test yourself against the competition, strategy takes shape in the determination to create value for customers' (Ohmae, 1988).

Most important, if the customer is the focus of attention, and performance is measured in terms of customer loyalty as well as overall spend, then risk management structures also need to reflect this philosophy. One simple example, of how this works in practice is the 'one in front' promise that no customer will have to queue behind more than one other in waiting for service at the checkout. Queues represent a risk that a customer will either walk out without buying, or wait but be reluctant to return and waste time waiting to be served. Risk is thus defined in very simple terms and this simplicity is one of the features of the Tesco approach.

Corporate culture

As indicated, the emphasis on the idea that the 'customer is king' has a direct impact upon the risk management system, because risk aversion is expressed in terms of doing the best one can for customers. In cultural terms, this is translated as 'we've all got a role to play' and Tesco staff purposely avoid talking about risk or a specific risk management function, and the creation of a risk department staffed by individuals taking on roles with risk related titles.

The feeling is that 'having a risk management function probably gets in the way of actually managing the risks because people are thinking about the risks as opposed to thinking about the customer, so all we are worried about is serving the customer and what can go wrong with that'. In other words, there is a danger that risk management cultures might actually get in the way of clear accountability for risk. 'This is about culture and terminology ... we don't want risk management to get in the way of what is a successful company, but we need to get risk management to dovetail into what we are trying to do'.

This cultural perspective was very clearly illustrated when an interviewee was asked about the perceived extent of risk awareness among the managers and operational staff. The response was 'I don't think in terms of the word risk there is one. I think, however, there is an awareness of things possibly going wrong'. In other words, the culture is one in which risk is defined and debated purely in terms of performance against objectives – and the core objective of serving the customer. Risk management and performance management are totally integrated, at least in terms of the underlying principles under which the business is managed.

This is an interesting contrast to the textbook view that risk management is a control system and that controls often create additional layers of bureaucracy. As the recent banking crisis has so vividly illustrated, risk management as a tick box exercise may actually be highly ineffective in control terms if people do not think about the underlying motivation behind the control. In its purest form, controls are put in place to help an organization achieve its objectives.

This culture does not imply that Tesco is devoid of formal structures for risk management – it is simply the case that the objectives of risk management are given precedence over the systems themselves. One simple way in which this idea can be seen to permeate the whole organization is via the creation of customer focused sound bites such as 'every little helps'. This is risk management in a subtle, rather than an elaborate form.

The nature of the business

The group has two business segments, retailing and financial services, with the former hugely dominant in terms of revenue, net assets and capital investment

Table 4.3 Business segments

Year ended 28 February 2009	Retailing £m	Financial services £m	Total £m
Revenue	54,164	163	54,327
Segment assets	39,788	6,203	45,991
Segment liabilities	(27,557)	(5,501)	(33,058)
Capital expenditure (including acquisitions through business combinations)	6,537	283	6,820

Source: Tesco Annual Report, 2009, p. 81

(Table 4.3). In essence, therefore, setting aside the financial services arm for the moment, Tesco is a fundamentally simple retail distribution business – albeit operating on a massive scale – that can be summarized in terms of five core processes:

- Buying products from suppliers.
- Sending them to a distribution centre.
- Transferring goods from the distribution centre to the stores.
- Taking cash.
- Banking the receipts.

The primary risks to the business are therefore those which threaten these processes. Not surprisingly, therefore, risk management in the business is built around process mapping which ensures a clear and detailed understanding of what factors might prevent processes running smoothly. Ultimately, 'Watching the supply chain is absolutely critical to ensure we are able to supply what the customer wants, when they want it, and in the condition they want'.

Organization structure

Complementing the relatively simple business model is a simple organizational structure which directly reflects it.

Despite employing almost 470,000 people around the globe, the grade structure in Tesco is relatively flat, as there are only five levels in the management hierarchy. The top two grades encompass approximately 200 people, and so the structure is a triangle with a very wide base. This flat structure offers, in principle, good opportunities for staff to progress through the hierarchy, and Sir Terence Leahy's profile provides evidence of this. He joined Tesco in 1979 after graduation as a marketing executive, and was appointed to the Board of Directors in 1992. Leahy became Chief Executive just five years later in 1997.

The flat structure makes it easier to identify accountability for risk, as risk registers cascade down the hierarchy, and risk management is made even more manageable by a structure that separates out the financial risks – managed by the

Treasury – from other risks which are overseen and monitored by internal audit. Additionally, Tesco Personal Finance (TPF) is run separately from the rest of the business, and until the buyout from Royal Bank of Scotland (RBS), the risks were shared between both parties to the joint venture. The customer model and branding belonged to Tesco but the infrastructure was that of RBS. (The management of risk in TPF is dealt with separately and in some depth later in this case study.)

Summary

The roots of the risk management system within Tesco lie in the corporate culture, business model and overall structure of the organization. In summary, risk is about performance management and performance is measured in terms of doing what the customer wants. The challenge is to make all of that work in practice by embedding risk awareness into the DNA of all staff. The next section explains the formal structures that are used to try and achieve this.

Governance

Overall structure

The governance structure within the group defines the way in which Tesco is directed and controlled. This structure is illustrated in Figure 4.1, which complements the narrative on governance that is contained with the annual report. The primary lines of accountability show the group Board of Directors overseeing the work of the Executive Committee[4] and boards of the various national subsidiaries, who in turn oversee the management teams in each country. The Retail Council, made up of around 40 people, is responsible for collecting together all the key decisions taken by the Board and the associated committees and cascading that information throughout the entire business. By using the retail council as the single conduit for core decisions, the risk of inconsistent messages is avoided.

The core structure is supported by a number of committees at both board level and below, each of which have a focused remit. The Board of Directors meets nine times a year, including a two-day off-site meeting to review strategy. The Executive Committee meets weekly and is responsible for implementing group strategy and policy and for monitoring the performance and compliance of the business, drawing on the work of relevant committees, and reporting on these matters in full to the Board.

At board level, the various strategic and regulatory committees deal with issues which are fundamental to the strategic success of Tesco and the protection of its reputation. These committees meet at varying intervals, but at least quarterly. Working together, they have responsibility for implementing the key elements of the group's strategic plan and managing its UK and international operations, joint ventures, property acquisitions, finance, funding and people

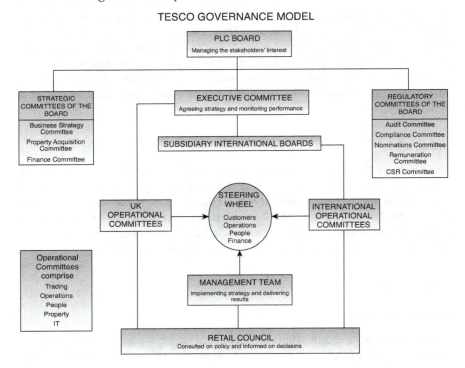

TESCO GOVERNANCE MODEL

Figure 4.1 Governance model
Source: Internal documentation provided by an interviewee

matters. The committees' members are a mix of Executive Directors and senior management from relevant functions.

Below board level, the operational committees are concerned with implementing the group's strategies and regulatory commitments at country level. The classification of the operational committees under the headings of trading, operations, people, property and IT offer insights into areas where the business feels risks need careful management. Trading is the heart of a retail business and operations; people, property and IT all feature in the Risks and Uncertainties section of the directors' report.

It is interesting to note that the governance structures covering international operations are identical to those covering the core UK market. This approach has two potential merits. First, it ensures consistency across the whole group, and second it facilitates the movement of staff across different geographic areas e.g. from Asia to Europe or vice versa, because the systems are common. In this way the valuable asset of senior staff can be utilized to maximum effect.

The steering wheel

At the centre of the governance structure is a steering wheel – Tesco's version of a balanced scorecard – which is the tool used for performance measurement and management against the targets laid down in the group's five year rolling plan. The 2009 version of the steering wheel is reproduced in Figure 4.2.

The five year plan establishes targets for the overall group, which reflect the core long term strategy of 'creating value for customers to earn their lifetime loyalty'. This is pursued through long-term growth of the business both in the UK and internationally. In the UK, growth is sought through expansion into markets such as financial services, non-food and telecoms. Internationally, growth is sought by entry into new locations, most recently China, India and the United States.

The strategies are used to generate plans and performance targets for each of the separate geographic and business segments. At all levels of Tesco – from group, through the business segments, national and regional operations, right down to the individual store, targets are also expressed in terms of the five perspectives of the steering wheel. At store level, the steering wheel is also linked

Figure 4.2 'Our steering wheel'
Source: Annual Report, 2009, p. 6

to the objectives of individual members of staff, so that group level strategies connect back to day-to-day work. When KPIs are not on track, systems are in place at every level of the organization to investigate the reasons why and to plan corrective action. Quarterly performance reports are submitted to the Board of Directors and a summary report is also sent to the group's top 2,000 managers for dissemination to staff.

Targets are defined under five separate perspectives of customers, operations, people, community and finance, which the company argues ensure that Tesco puts 'appropriate balance' into the trade-offs that need to be made between the main elements of customer metrics, financial measures and operational efficiency and effectiveness. They argue that for the shareholders, the balanced approach is beneficial because the combination of operational efficiency and customers who are well looked after will combine to improve sales, profits and investor returns. The idea that an improved financial performance is the outcome of good perform-ance in the areas of customers, operations and people approach is very closely aligned with that of Kaplan and Norton, who first promoted the balanced score-card approach. The cycle is driven by paying very close attention to the customer's needs, which when satisfied creates a virtuous circle of improving results as shown below in Figure 4.3. This focus on the customer fits with the widely accepted principle that increased customer loyalty is the single most important driver of long term financial performance (Norreklit, 2000).

Proving the empirical existence of this virtuous circle is almost impossible because of all of the intervening factors that may impact on performance. That said, the steering wheel has been in place in Tesco since 2005 and over that period group revenues have increased by over 50 per cent; the gross operating margin has remained constant and EPS has increased by 75 per cent. This would suggest that the strategies are proving successful from a shareholder perspective and the steering wheel does work to improve performance, at least for this organization.

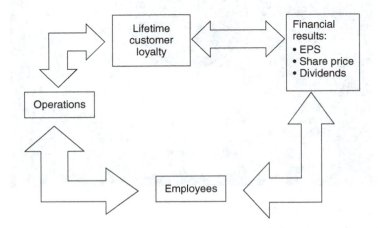

Figure 4.3 Cause and effect in the steering wheel.

The steering wheel is used to monitor and control performance in relation to each of the five elements and KPIs relating to shareholders are tracked by monitoring both total shareholder return and the full year dividend per share. Some, but not all of the KPIs for the group are detailed in the Directors' Report (Table 4.4). Each business across the group is required to report performance against the steering wheel targets on a quarterly basis, although trading figures are reviewed daily and weekly. The steering wheel for the group is reviewed quarterly.

Staff commitment to the steering wheel and associated targets is encouraged in two separate ways. The first is by the application of a process referred to internally as 'Values', which are used to ensure that every member of staff around the world understands the group's culture and goals. The values are summarized as:

- No one tries harder for customers:
  - Understand customers.
  - Be first to meet their needs.
  - Act responsibly for our communities.
- We treat people how we like to be treated ...
  - Work as a team.
  - Trust and respect each other.
  - Listen, support and say thank you.
  - Share knowledge and experience.
- ... so we can enjoy our work.

The second way of encouraging staff commitment to targets is by the use of a number of schemes designed to encourage their involvement in the financial

Table 4.4 Key performance indicators

Financial	Customers	Operations	People	Community, including environment
Sales growth Trading margin	n.a.	UK market share: grocery UK market share: non-food	Employee retention rate (more than one year)	Reduction in CO_2 emissions overall Reduction in CO_2 emissions per square foot in new stores
Net cash inflow/outflow Capital investment Net borrowings Gearing Return on capital employed Underlying dilutes EPS Total shareholder return Total annual dividend				

performance of the group. Performance against targets is closely linked to remuneration at the level of the executive directors, and there is also a profit sharing scheme in place for all employees with more than one year's service with the company. The executive bonus scheme offers both long- and short-term bonuses, paid in a mix of cash and share options. Payment is linked to the achievement of a mix of targets covering EPS growth, ROCE growth, total shareholder return and the achievement of specific, but confidential, strategic goals. Employees receive a profit share that is calculated pro-rata to their base salary, up to the maximum £3,000 annual tax free limit set by the Revenue and Customs, and may also opt to participate in a savings-related share option scheme and a partnership share plan.[5]

Making it work

Clearly articulated strategies and a structured set of performance targets encompassing both financial and non-financial aspects of the organization create a framework that should at least encourage, if not ensure, that all staff across the group are aware of and make efforts to achieve the core objectives. Risk creates a threat to the achievement of these objectives and therefore aims are only achieved to the full if risks are effectively recognized, controlled and monitored. Linking risk management to performance management is vital to make the whole thing work.

Linking risk management to performance management

Basic principles

> One of the reasons we are a successful company is because of risk management – people do it without actually knowing they are doing it, it's part of their accountabilities. They are held to account. We monitor things on such a micro level.
>
> (Interviewee)

This is a fascinating summary of Tesco's approach to risk management, which provides a stark contrast to the seemingly bureaucratic structures of risk management that have evolved in some global financial institutions that have still ultimately failed. At the heart of Tesco's approach is the idea that performance management and risk management run hand in hand, and so if people focus on performance targets then they are simultaneously but *implicitly* managing their risks.

The risk management standard produced by the Institute of Risk Management (2002) identifies three key elements in the risk management process, namely risk assessment, risk reporting and risk response (measures to reduce or modify risks), and all three elements form part of a control loop that is used by Tesco to ensure complementarities between the risk management controls and the

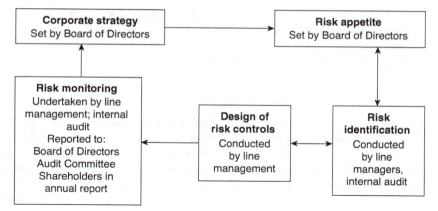

Figure 4.4 Linking strategy to performance to risk management

performance targets set within the steering wheel. The control loop is portrayed in Figure 4.4.

The control loop shows that the process begins with the specification of corporate strategy by the Board of Directors, the identification of key risks and the associated risk appetite of the group. At lower levels of the organization, risk identification is the responsibility of line management, assisted by advice from internal audit. Risk responses and control mechanisms are also the responsibility of line management and internal audit then independently monitors the risk systems that have been established. Internal audit report their findings on internal control back to the Audit Committee and Board of Directors and may also offer advice to line managers regarding deficiencies or potential improvements to risk controls. Under the existing corporate governance regulations the Board of Directors is also required to report that it has conducted a review of the effectiveness of the internal controls. In the case of Tesco, the Directors' Report also includes a statement that the controls in place remain appropriate. The risk reporting process then feeds back into the strategy setting process to inform and possibly modify future plans for the business.

Roles and responsibilities for risk: the board of directors and senior management

The board of directors has overall responsibility for risk management and internal control within the context of achieving the group's overall objectives. In practical terms this means that the Board's role is threefold:

Setting the group's risk appetite

The risk appetite is set in the light of the directors' views about market and shareholder requirements and the need to balance risk controls with the facility to seize opportunities. The risk appetite will also be influenced by global economic conditions, the existing business mix and the known associated risks. In terms of the broader business, the risk controls that are established must ensure that the risks taken mirror the risk appetite of the board.

Identifying the key risks facing the group

Key risks may be defined as those which threaten core strategies. The Key Risk Register, maintained by Internal Audit, is built up/revised through regular discussion between members of the Board of Directors, the Executive Committee and other senior managers. In addition, there is an annual Board meeting dedicated to a review of the strategic risks across all of the businesses. The resulting risk register contains information not just on the nature of the risk(s) but also their potential impact and likelihood, and the register is updated on an ongoing basis through feedback from a range of sources, including the steering wheel. All risks are allocated to a named 'owner' and the controls and procedures used to mitigate them are identified.

A list and summary description of key risks facing the group is contained within the corporate governance section of the annual report (pp. 38–40). The list covers a total of 19 categories including business strategy, financial strategy, financial services (through Tesco Personal Finance), operational, joint venture, property, health and safety and environmental risks and it is too long to be very informative. The significance of the risks listed may vary widely, and also change over time but some major risks stand out. One example of a key risk is that of both regulatory and public attitudes towards large retailers. Changes to planning rules could severely impede the group's strategy for growth, and so risk management involves putting in place mechanisms that can be used to quickly respond to and mitigate changes in planning rules. The use of political lobbying will be one response, accompanied by changes in the format of stores, such as shifting to smaller sites, especially in town centres where other stores are closing down.

Another way of viewing key risks is to pinpoint the factors on which the strategy depends. Earlier, it was suggested that Tesco is a simple business based around six core processes. The key risks are therefore those which threaten the effectiveness of those processes: 'The Tesco philosophy is "the customer is king": without the customer we don't exist. Every part of that process is customer oriented. ... What that means is that the things that we would be looking for is ... we would be watching the service–supply chain'.

A highly efficient and effective supply chain requires investment in IT systems and procurement and delivery infrastructures. As the annual report notes:

> The business is dependent on efficient information technology (IT) systems. Any significant failure in the IT processes of our retail operations (e.g. barcode scanning or supply chain logistics) would impact our ability to trade. We recognize the essential role that IT plays across our operations in

allowing us to trade efficiently and so that we can achieve commercial advantage through implementing IT innovations that improve the shopping trip for customers and make life easier for employees. We have extensive controls in place to maintain the integrity and efficiency of our IT infrastructure and we share systems from across our international operations to ensure consistency of delivery.

(Tesco Annual Report, p. 39)

Overseeing the group's risk and internal control system

The Board is responsible for the overall system of internal control and for reviewing the effectiveness of such a system. The annual report states that group-wide processes are in place for establishing the risks and responsibilities assigned to each level of management and the controls which are required to be implemented and monitored. The control system is designed to mitigate against the risk of not achieving objectives, rather than to totally eliminate the risk of failure. As such, it is acknowledged that some activities carry risks which are outside the Board's control.

Responsibility for the annual review of the effectiveness of the internal control systems rests with the Audit Committee which meets quarterly and reports directly to the Board. The Audit Committee can also be more proactive in their management of risks, and will sometimes take trips to inspect overseas operations and gain an on-site view of internal control. The Committee, chaired by a non-executive director, receives regular reports from the Head of Internal Audit on internal control effectiveness and also has the power to take action to call senior line managers to account if it believes they are failing in their risk management duties. If, for example, a national CEO has been a bit slower in managing risk than the Audit Committee might like him/her to have been, the CEO may be flown over for a meeting – 'a bit like being in the headmaster's study' – to explain what is happening and why.

Two other senior management committees also play an important role in monitoring the exposure to risk and effectiveness of internal controls. Regulatory risk management falls under the eye of the Compliance Committee, which meets six times a year with the remit to ensure that the group complies with all the necessary laws and regulations in all of its operations worldwide. Risk management within the Treasury and tax functions are subject to review by the Finance Committee, which also sets the Treasury limits.

Roles and responsibilities for risk: Internal Audit

The internal audit function is independent of business operations and works across the entire group to evaluate and monitor the internal control and risk management processes. The staff see their role as one of facilitation. Their primary customer is the Audit Committee, and their primary service is to the Board in giving them assurance that the risks faced by the business are adequately managed and covered, and in line with the Board's declared risk appetite.

The audit plan is risk-based, and largely focused around the six core processes that dictate the success of the core strategy. There is also a list of items that are audited automatically, such as new ventures, third-party risks, and areas where the business is not building as it should. This fits with the findings of Selim and McNamee (1999), who found that the assets, projects and processes that were deemed key to strategic objectives were central to the definition of the audit universe. The audit programme thus focuses on perceived 'problem' areas and new businesses where risks are less well understood. Managerial experience and intuition is used to identify the problem areas – 'at the end of the day it is people's experience and how you feel' (Head of Internal Audit). This approach matches that found by Helliar *et al.* (2002), who found that judgements based on experience were preferred to probabilistic measures of risk.

For each audit, all of the potential risks of the chosen process are identified, together with information on what controls are in place to mitigate those risks. The result is a process risk map in a form similar to a flow chart (Box 4.1).

The detail of how internal audit works is best understood via a more detailed example, of an audit of site acquisition in a central European country. Site acquisition is clearly a key process that will affect the ability of Tesco to achieve its growth targets (Box 4.2).

Staff in Internal Audit come from a mix of backgrounds, some CIMA, ACCA or ICAEW qualified but also some with Institute of Internal Auditors' qualifications and the churn rate within the department is quite high. This is seen as beneficial because when staff move from internal audit into other areas of the business they take an awareness of risk management with them.

Around 25 per cent of activities/processes are audited each year and the resulting reports are non-standard and clearly specify the next steps to be taken, and who is responsible for them. The reports get sent through to the Board member responsible for the particular area, and depending upon the time scale, internal audit will probably return in due course to review if actions have been taken as required. Line management remuneration and sometimes survival, is dependent upon them fulfilling the actions required of them.

The head of internal audit reports directly to the head of the Audit Committee (a non-executive manager), and also attends all of that committee's meetings.

Box 4.1 Process risk mapping for internal audit

Key steps:

1   Identify the risks and the factors that may trigger them.
2   Identify the current controls that are in place.
3   Evaluate control effectiveness by reference back to the organizational risk appetite.

Box 4.2 Internal audit of overseas site acquisition

An auditor will pick up an area – this is site acquisition in X, for example. We have a property specialist put together the typical risks that you would get in a property process, so he would put together an overall risk thing. The auditor will go and have a talk to senior management and to the people involved in the process and will then adjust the risk model to reflect the risks specific to that country's business, anything that could go wrong. He then goes along to the business and literally starts working through: 'First of all, tell me what you do and how you do it, then show me what you do and show me how you do it', and he'll actually look at the documents and everything else. So he would say in the case of 'failure to identify all potential sites of interest on the market,' 'So how do you ensure that you do identify all of the potential sites on the market?' And they'll say, 'Oh well, we do a strategy review of this, we do this, we do ...' and so on and so forth. You'll then be talking to some of the property specialists in Hungary who are outside of the business and saying, 'Right, is there anything the company isn't doing?' The auditor can then report back on whether he thinks it is adequately controlled or not. A recommendation then comes out, which is the responsibility of the line manager to implement.

If a risk is deemed significant enough, it may appear on the key risk register, and is reported to the Board as well as the Audit Committee.

In addition, he/she reports to an executive manager – the PLC Finance and Strategy Director on a day-to-day basis.

Roles and responsibilities for risk: line management and other staff

As already indicated, risk is seen as the responsibility of all staff, as reflected in the performance targets set within the steering wheel. The risk management process is cascaded through the group with every international CEO and local Boards maintaining their own risk registers and assessing their control systems. The same process also applies functionally in those parts of the group requiring greater oversight (Tesco, 2009, p. 48). For example, key risks are identified for HR and distribution as these are seen as core functions.

Accountability of the CEOs of subsidiary businesses is attained via a requirement for them to issue annual statements of assurance that the Board's governance policies have been adopted both in practice and in spirit. In some, but not all, joint ventures e.g. TPF pre-2008, the Board's assurance is dependent upon the internal control systems of the partner and the obligations upon their Boards relating to the effectiveness of their own systems.

Within the broader management base, a number of key groups at national level carry significant responsibility for risk management. The governance model in Figure 4.1 shows a number of operational committees – trading, operations, people, property and IT – each with a remit to manage a specific area of risk. Performance against steering wheel targets, and the findings of internal audit reviews are reported to these committees, although the ultimate responsibility for controlling the risks rests with line management.

Every store has a steering wheel, and where performance is below expected the wheel is marked red, and risk awareness is defined in terms of not hitting the steering wheel targets, rather than the term 'risk' per se. When asked about the extent of risk awareness amongst store staff the following exchange with one interviewee is very revealing:

> *Interviewee*: I don't think the word risk, there is one, I think how far is there an awareness of things possibly going wrong, and then how do they control things going wrong. I think there is a very high …
> *Researcher*: And that extends to the shelf fillers?
> *Interviewee*: Yes it does, yes, even if it's just that they know that they don't meet the five o'clock clear up time or something.

What this reveals is the point made much earlier in this case – that risk management is *implicit* within performance management in Tesco – it does not simply constitute an additional layer of bureaucracy.

The risk management framework

As already indicated, the risk management framework employed in Tesco closely matches that of the risk standard developed by the Institute of Risk Management (2002) illustrated in Figure 4.5.

Box 4.3 Example: monitoring price risk

The target is to offer the lowest price to customers whilst taking relative quality into account. Monitoring is done by *daily* review of the price of an industry-typical basket of goods. If prices are proving unfavourable, somebody is charged – that day – with finding out why.

Risk is measured in terms of actual price differential, e.g. £37.64 versus £38.30, and members of the operations committee for the relevant country meet weekly to discuss the observed differential. The meeting can select to accept prices as OK or adjust them but either way the maximum time lag to react is just one week. This is short because price competitiveness is critical to the group's strategy.

Figure 4.5 Core elements of the risk management process
Source: Adapted from Institute of Risk Management (2002)

Risk assessment and evaluation is done by line management, using a risk and materiality matrix which classifies risks as green, amber or red dependent upon a combination of likelihood and consequences. The categorization is based upon experience and 'gut feeling' rather than detailed risk modelling, but provides a basis for identifying which risks are worthy of greater or lesser monitoring. For example, in terms of financial control, the finance manager may identify the risks faced as including:

- Cash management.
- Investment appraisal.
- Balance sheet control.
- Financial information systems.
- Skill risks (shortage of key people).
- Managing the 'City'.
- Compliance with IFRS.
- Financing, e.g. illiquidity.
- Re-financing.
- Interest rates.
- Foreign exchange.
- Counterparty credit.
- Tax.

All of the above risks have owners and all are classed as green, amber or red. Red implies the risk is a glaring problem. Amber means 'we aren't comfortable with where we are at on the risk scale but we do have a plan to tackle it'. Green is that 'we are comfortable with the risk that we are taking.' The risk owner is required to take action to bring the risk level down to green wherever possible, and advice on how to do this will be provided by internal audit.

The risk registers, allocation of risk ownership and action plans all form important parts of the risk management process, but ultimately risks are only managed if the process is continuous, and this requires that the risks and action plans are the subject of regular review. The frequency of monitoring reflects the level of significance of the risk.

Risk reporting and communication

Figure 4.5 portrays the lines of communication used within Tesco PLC. The arrows indicate the direction of the information flow, with upward arrows showing reporting lines, whilst downward arrows show the communication of objectives or priorities. Risk issues are reported to the specialist monitoring committees and internal audit. Internal audit reports to the audit committee, the members of which may also 'drive' internal audit, or the actions of line managers via the expression of concerns over areas of business where risk is being controlled inadequately.

Note, Figure 4.6 is my personal interpretation of the communication lines used within Tesco. It is intended to complement the governance model that is used internally by the group as is depicted in Figure 4.1.

As already indicated, in the interviews the business was described as being relatively shallow, with only five grades of staff from top to bottom. This indirectly assists in the communication process. The formal lines of communication are also augmented by informal systems that are used to further the achievement of objectives. For example, one interviewee observed that 'many years ago we decided on a strategy of trying to improve the controls of the business by getting as many people as we could [who] trained through audit'. 'Spread the message' communication is therefore achieved via a number of complementary routes.

At the same time, the involvement of operational managers in the identification of risks helps the process of risk communication across the whole group, and fits with De Haas and Kleingeld's (1999) suggestion that participation is vital to the effectiveness of a control system. All risks are owned and exposure is clear under the traffic light system. Consequently, because the risk reporting lines go right through from line management up to the Board of Directors, no business or individual escapes scrutiny.

The big challenge: extending the risk management system into Tesco Personal Finance

TPF is the UK's largest supermarket bank, and was established 12 years ago as a joint venture with Royal Bank of Scotland (RBS). Following the financial losses at RBS, Tesco bought out its share of the joint venture in July 2008 for the sum of £950 million, and it has recently moved to new headquarters in Edinburgh.

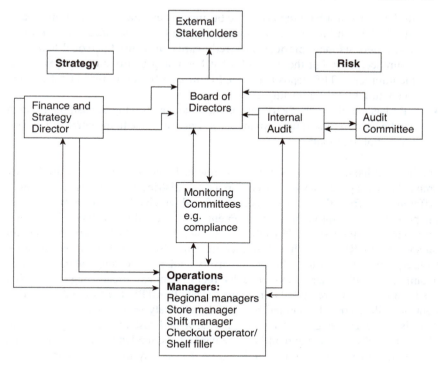

Figure 4.6 Communication lines in Tesco

The shift from a 50 per cent share in a joint venture to 100 per cent ownership of a financial services business fits well with Tesco's declared long term strategy of growth via investment in retailing services such as Tesco.com, telecoms and financial services. The transfer of the group's Finance Director to the role of Chief Executive of Retailing Services in July 2008 might be viewed as an indicator of the level of significance that this market holds for Tesco. Sir Terence Leahy believes that the recent banking failures have played into Tesco's hands and provided them with an opportunity to expand retail services from its current position of £400 million profit to in excess of £1 billion within a decade. Press reports suggest that Tesco has been strengthening its financial services arm since 2008 by taking advantage of the financial crisis to take its pick of banking experts. At the same time, analysts such as Clive Black at Shore Capital forecast that Tesco Personal Finance could triple its revenues to £600 million within the next five years.

On a number of levels, the risks associated with expansion of its financial services arm appear relatively low because:

- TPF is a 'known animal' given the company's ten years of experience in the joint venture.

- In the midst of a banking crisis the business is expanding its customer base. In mid-2009 it had 6 million accounts in the UK, compared with 5 million a year ago; its main products are credit cards, unsecured personal loans and insurance, although there is talk of it beginning to offer mortgages in the medium term. TPF deposits doubled from £2.5 billion in mid-October 2008 to about £4.5 billion in July 2009.
- TPF has a high level of earnings retention and a growing deposit base which can be used to fund future expansion without recourse to the currently expensive wholesale markets.

On the other hand, in terms of risk management, Tesco is entering an entirely new arena. The core processes which support a retail distribution business carry rather different risks from the financial risks associated with banking. Furthermore, over the period of the joint venture arrangement, Tesco relied upon RBS's infrastructure to manage the risks within TPF. Even now, most of TPF's operations remain outsourced to RBS, which in itself carries the risk of lack of direct control. Consequently, the group's finance, treasury and internal audit teams need to acquire new skills. There is evidence that recruitment has already begun, but even if specialist staff are recruited to manage risks within TPF, the associated internal controls will need to be audited by Tesco's relatively small internal audit team. This is a big challenge and it will provide a real test of the group's current philosophy of risk management because banks have tended to bureaucratize and silo the risk management function, isolating it from day-to-day operations. Such an approach runs directly counter to Tesco's current style of risk management and so the next two or three years will be very interesting. If revenues continue to grow and profit margins remain intact, then Tesco may really have found the holy grail of how to manage risk. If not ... ?

Conclusion

At the start of this case, risk management was defined as the 'process of understanding and managing the risks that the entity is inevitably subject to in attempting to achieve its corporate objectives'. The case provides evidence that Tesco seeks to engender understanding of risk amongst its staff by expressing risk in terms of performance targets. Additionally, those targets – via the steering wheel – encompass customers, people, the community and operations as well as the more common financial objectives.

In a company as large as Tesco, which is now the world's third largest retailer, it would be easy for objectives and targets to be misinterpreted but risk is contained by keeping the messages simple. It is not difficult for any staff member to recall that 'the customer is king' and 'every little helps'. If rewards are also available for those who do remember, and they get a share of company profits, then the risks of owners being divorced from controllers is minimized. In summary, Tesco's risk management system is characterized by simplicity – corporate strategies which are simply expressed; a business model that, until recently, depended upon just six core processes, and a culture that views risk management as an integral part of performance management rather than an additional layer of bureaucracy. Perhaps sometimes, simplest is best.

References

CIMA (2005) *Official Terminology*, CIMA Publishing/Elsevier, Oxford.

De Haas, M. and Kleingeld, A. (1999) 'Multilevel design of performance measurement systems: enhancing strategic dialogue throughout the organisation', *Management Accounting Research*, Vol. 10, pp. 233–61.

Helliar, C. V., Lomie, A. A., Power, D. and Sinclair, C. D. (2002) Managerial attitudes to risk: a comparison of Scottish chartered accountants and UK managers', *Journal of International Accounting, Auditing and Taxation*, Vol. 11, pp. 156–90.

Institute of Risk Management (2002) *A Risk Management Standard*, IRM, London.

Norreklit, H. (2000) 'The balance on the balanced scorecard – a critical analysis of some of its assumptions', *Management Accounting Research*, Vol. 11, pp. 65–88.

Ohmae, K. (1988) 'Getting back to strategy', *Harvard Business Review*, Vol. 66, No. 6, pp. 149–56.

Selim, G. and McNamee, D. (1999) 'The risk management and internal auditing relationship: developing and validating a model', *International Journal of Auditing*, Vol. 3, pp. 159–74.

Tesco (2009) Annual Report and Financial Statements.

5 Case study
Royal Bank of Scotland

Company profile

History

The Royal Bank of Scotland was founded in Edinburgh in 1727. By 1900 it had over 130 branches in Scotland and had opened its first branch in London. During the 1920s and 1930s it established a significant presence in England through the acquisition of Glyn Mills and Williams Deacon's. By 1970, having merged with the National Commercial Bank of Scotland, it was the leading bank in Scotland, with over 700 branches.

During the 1980s RBS diversified its business, pioneering the direct distribution of motor insurance through the establishment of Direct Line in 1985, and entering US banking in 1988 with the acquisition of Citizens Bank of Rhode Island.

In the 1990s RBS refocused on its core retail banking business and acquired the private bank of Adam & Co. Direct Banking was launched in 1994, and it rapidly became the UK's fastest growing 24-hour telephone banking service. In 1997 RBS launched the UK's first comprehensive internet banking service, as well as financial services operations in partnership with Virgin and Tesco. In combination, these developments marked the move away from branch-based banking into a broader format for service provision.

In 2000 RBS completed the £21 billion acquisition of NatWest (including Ulster Bank), the biggest take-over in British banking history. The result was a group with over 20 million customers, £400 billion assets and 110,000 employees worldwide. Since the acquisition of NatWest, RBS has continued to pursue a strategy of both organic growth and growth through acquisitions.

In the United States, Citizens' Bank expanded from New England into the mid-Atlantic states through the acquisition of the Mellon Bank regional franchise, and into the Midwest though the acquisition of Charter One, completed in 2004. The following year, RBS purchased a 5 per cent stake in the Bank of China at a cost of £1.7 billion but the Bank of China shares were sold again in January 2009 for £1.6 billion. In insurance, the acquisition of Churchill meant that RBS is now the second largest general insurer in the UK and in corporate banking the group now operates across the United States, European and Asia Pacific markets.

Press comment in the period after the NatWest purchase suggested that 'few of the acquisitions made the same kind of sense',[1] but in 2007 RBS spent a further £10 billion for its share of the Dutch bank ABN AMRO, as part of a consortium with the Belgian bank Fortis and Spanish Banco Santander. At the time, many commentators regarded the deal as being overly aggressive and overpriced. In evidence to the 2009 Treasury Select Committee on the banking crisis, the former chairman, Sir Tom McKillop, noted that the entire value of the goodwill in the acquisition has subsequently had to be written off.

The Group has been extremely adversely affected by the financial crisis, to the extent that it has moved from being the fifth largest bank in the world by market capitalization in 2006 to one which in February 2009 posted a loss of £24.1 billion for the previous financial year. This is the largest annual loss in British corporate history. In 2009 HM Treasury took a 70 per cent controlling shareholding and RBS was also the first bank to sign up to the UK government's asset protection plan. The bank has moved £325 billion of illiquid assets from its global markets division into the plan, in exchange for the issue to the government of two blocks of preference shares.

In 2009 RBS began a rationalization and restructuring programme, which included withdrawing from 36 of the 54 countries within which it operates, cutting jobs, selling off assets and eliminating bonuses for most of the senior staff. It remains to be seen how long, if ever, it will take to regain the huge amount of shareholder value that has been destroyed over the last few years.

Stock market listings

London Stock Exchange; New York Stock Exchange (ADRs).

Core divisions and brands

*   *Global Banking and Markets* (GBM). GBM provides a range of debt and equity financing, risk management and investment services to corporate customers.
*   *Global Transaction Services*. This division provides transaction services to companies in the areas of global payments, cash and liquidity management, trade finance, and United Kingdom and international merchant card products and services. It includes the Group's corporate money transmission activities in the United Kingdom and the United States.
*   *UK Retail and Commercial Banking*. This division represents the core of the RBS Group. In the retail market, RBS UK serves over 15 million personal customers through the RBS and NatWest brands. It offers a full range of banking products and related financial services including mortgages, deposit accounts, and credit and charge cards. *Brands:* RBS, NatWest, Coutts, Adam & Co., RBS International and NatWest Offshore.
*   *US Retail and Commercial Banking*. US Retail and Commercial Banking provides financial services primarily through the Citizens and Charter One brands.

- *Europe and Middle East Retail and Commercial Banking.* Europe and Middle East Retail and Commercial Banking comprises Ulster Bank and the group's combined retail and commercial businesses in Europe and the Middle East. Ulster Bank remains a core part of the Group's global banking operations but the E&ME Retail and Commercial franchises outside Ireland lack scale and breadth. Consequently, the group has commenced a review to consider future options for these businesses, including options for sale.
- *Asia Retail and Commercial Banking.* Asia Retail and Commercial Banking is present in markets including India, Pakistan, China, Taiwan, Hong Kong, Indonesia, Malaysia and Singapore. It provides financial services across four segments: affluent banking, cards and consumer finance, business banking and international wealth management.
  The group intends to exit its retail and commercial activities in these areas, although RBS Coutts, operating in the field of wealth management, will remain a core business.
- *RBS Insurance.* RBS Insurance is the UK's second largest general insurer and the largest personal lines insurer by gross written premiums. It sells and underwrites personal loans and SME insurance over the telephone and internet, as well as through brokers, RBS Group bank branches and partnerships. *Brands include:* Direct Line, Churchill and Privilege, NIG, Green Flag.

Sources of data reported in the case study

The material used in the case study is drawn from a number of different sources, but primarily upon internal documentation from the company and interview

Table 5.1 RBS: key financial statistics

Statistic	Year ending 31 December		
	1999	2004	2008
Revenue (£ million)	1,756	9,208	18,675
• Net interest income	1,672	13,546	867
• Non-interest income (excluding insurance)	710	4,944	6,326
• Insurance income (net of reinsurance)			
• Total	4,138	22,754	25,868
Cost–income ratio (group) (%)	49.5	40.8	208.9[a]
Profit before taxation (£ million)	1,211	6,917	(40,700)
Earnings per share (£0.01)	87.8	172.5	(61)
Return on equity post-tax (%)	32	20.1	Nil
Total assets (£ million)	88,900	583,467	2,401,652
Full time equivalent employees	32,670	136,600	197,100

Note: [a] Includes capital market write downs and one-off items. Excluding these, the figure is 59.2%.

transcripts. In preparation for the interviews, publicly available information on the risk management system and practices was reviewed.

The core data was collected in the period preceding the banking crisis, but it is a longitudinal study that tracks changes in thinking and the evolution of the systems within Royal Bank of Scotland (RBS) over a four-year time frame up to the start of 2007. For the sake of completeness, the case is extended to include an analysis of publicly available data post 2007 which is used to identify changes to the risk management and internal control systems that have occurred in response to the crisis.

Key observations

The case provides evidence that:

- Effective control requires the incorporation of the vital element of human judgement to add value to mechanistic measurement and reporting structures.
- Assuming that high levels of leverage will increase shareholder value may encourage excessive risk taking.
- Large and complex businesses with a portfolio of interdependent risks face major problems in measuring and managing aggregate risks, and concepts such as Enterprise Risk Management potentially underestimate such problems.

Introduction

Sir Tom McKillop, former Chairman of RBS Group PLC and Sir Fred Goodwin, former Chief Executive of RBS Group PLC were faced with the following questions from the Chairman when they appeared before the House of Commons Treasury Committee during the banking crisis:

> In my preparation for this I looked up the *Oxford English Dictionary* definition of a 'bank'. It says: 'An organization offering financial services, especially the safe keeping of customers' money until required and making loans at interest'. Does that definition need updating? Do we need to contact the *Oxford English Dictionary* again? … Did your organization live up to that definition?'

These very challenging questions go to the heart of the problems facing risk managers in the banking sector:

- How does the risk management function in banks balance the need to protect depositors' money, with the need to earn profits for shareholders? In essence, is risk management a function designed to protect from risk or to encourage entrepreneurial risk taking?

- What is a bank? In the twenty-first century it is much more than a deposit taker and issuer of loans, but the growing complexity of financial services makes the risk management of such services also more complex.

This case study cannot hope to provide definitive answers to these questions, but what it does seek to do is to provide some detail about the context within which the risk management function at RBS operates and the structures created to manage risks.

External influences on risk management in banks

Governance regulations

Private sector organizations have been strongly encouraged to formalize their risk management systems as a result of international corporate governance regulations which require the establishment of effective internal control procedures. There are two different forms of regulation. First, those given the power of law, as under the Sarbanes Oxley Act in the United States and the associated SEC rules. Second, those regulations developed by private standard setters as part of a corporate governance code e.g. the Combined Code in the UK, or Australian Principles of Good Governance and Best Practice.

In the United States, the Sarbanes Oxley Act (SOX) emerged in 2003 as a response to a spate of corporate disasters including the implosion of Long Term Capital Management in 1998, Enron in December 2001, and WorldCom in 2002. SOX forced members of the boards of directors of companies to become much more risk aware, and under Section 404 of the Act, a company's SEC filing must include an internal control report which states management's responsibility for maintaining an adequate internal control procedure for financial reporting, together with an assessment of its effectiveness. The SEC do not mandate the use of a specific single framework for the control system, but indicate the suitability of any of the following:

- COSO (1992) guidelines (updated via COSO 2004).
- Guidance on Assessing Control, Canadian Institute of Chartered Accountants.
- Turnbull Report (UK).

It is important to note, however, that the SEC do not prescribe a methodology for the evaluation of effectiveness as circumstances will vary from company to company. In addition, the emphasis is on internal controls relating to financial reporting, rather than broader risk management objectives.

The New York Stock Exchange listing rules further reiterate the view that responsibility for risk assessment and management rests on the CEO and senior management (NYSE Listed Company Manual, Corporate Governance Standards, s. 303.A.07(D)).

Box 5.1 Internal control

The board should maintain a sound system of internal control to safeguard shareholders' investment and the company's assets.

Code provision

C.2.1 The board should, at least annually, conduct a review of the effectiveness of the group's system of internal controls and should report to shareholders that they have done so. The review should cover all material controls, including financial, operational and compliance controls and risk management system.

(Section C2, 'Combined Code', FRC, 2006, p. 14)

In the UK, under the Combined Code (FRC, 2006) the Board of Directors of listed companies[2] accept responsibility for the system of internal financial control and for monitoring its effectiveness – see Box 5.1. The code suggests the use of the revised Turnbull Report (FRC, 2005) as a useful guide on how to establish a risk management framework and evaluate its effectiveness.

Banks all around the world are therefore pushed into paying attention to risk management as part of a broader process of improving corporate governance. This pressure is reinforced by the international banking regulations.

Banking regulation

There is strong evidence that banking regulation has played an important role in making banks more aware of the risks they are taking (Hull, 2007). This is not to say that the regulations have been wholly effective, but simply that they have acted as an influence.

One form of regulation which has influenced bank behaviour and risk management arose out of the need for banks to behave in a way that protects their depositors' money, as raised in the Treasury Committee question quoted above. Governments around the world have established regulations which provide for a level of deposit insurance which helps to reassure depositors that their money is safe. One side effect of such insurance, however, is that it can serve to encourage banks to hold very low levels of equity capital, in order to increase the returns on equity. The capital structure of banks, in which equity capital is often very low relative to the assets on the balance sheet, is a major source of risk as demonstrated so clearly in the recent financial crisis.

In 1988 the international regulators responded to this potential risk problem by establishing capital adequacy ratios under the Basel Accord. The Basel regulations specified the amount of capital a bank needed to hold according to the perceived riskiness of its activities: higher risk assets needed to be supported by more capital. The Basel rules have since been updated and amended and a final set of revised rules – the Basel II Capital Requirements – were published in 2004 and took effect in 2007 (BIS, 2005).

Basel II is made up of three 'pillars':

- Minimum capital requirements.
- Supervisory review.
- Market discipline.

Minimum capital requirements are set for each of three classes of risk – credit, market and operational – although the precise details of how this is done are outside the scope of this case study.[3] The minimum aggregate capital requirement for a bank is the sum of all three. As the case study will demonstrate, this split into specific risk categories strongly influences the way in which the risk management function is structured within banks such as RBS.

Banking supervisors, via supervisory review, are regarded as playing an important role in ensuring compliance with the capital requirements and are also tasked with encouraging banks to evaluate and improve their risk management systems. In the UK, the Financial Services Authority is responsible for the supervision of banks and financial services, and it adopts a risk-based approach to its role.[4] The system used by the FSA to assess the risk within firms is termed the ARROW framework. ARROW stands for the Advanced, Risk-Responsive Operating FrameWork, the first version of which was published in 2003, but has now been replaced by ARROW II issued in 2006 (FSA, 2003, 2006 for full details).

The ARROW assessment categorizes firms under one of four risk headings which combine likelihood and impact assessments. Figure 5.1 shows the mix of firms in each category as of August 2006.

The high risk group of 95 institutions (including RBS) is made up of the UK's largest banks and groups, where failure or liquidity problems could have a substantive impact upon the wider economy.

The frequency and depth of regulatory review directly reflects the risk categorization of a bank, and is annual for the highest risk levels. The review may involve a complete assessment of all business and control risks within the firm (Full ARROW) or a reduced scope risk assessment (Light ARROW) covering core issues only. The core areas of assessment are as follows:

For all firms –

- Management, governance and culture.
- Control functions.
- Capital and liquidity.

For firms with significant retail business –

- Customers, products (and markets).

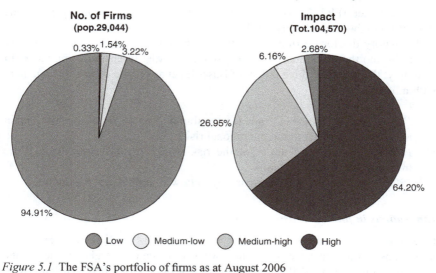

No. of Firms
(pop.29,044)

Impact
(Tot.104,570)

0.33% 1.54% 3.22%

6.16%   2.68%

26.95%

94.91%

64.20%

○ Low   ○ Medium-low   ○ Medium-high   ● High

Figure 5.1 The FSA's portfolio of firms as at August 2006
Source: Adapted from FSA (2006), p. 17

For firms with significant wholesale business:

• Customers, products (and markets).

For firms with permission to hold or control client money:

• Client money.

The core elements of ARROW include both the Supervisory Review and the associated assessment of Capital Adequacy under the Basel II capital requirements. Discussion of the details of how the Basel II supervisory processes are applied falls outside the scope of this study, but can be found in 'Our Pillar II Assessment Framework' (FSA, 2007).

For all banks, a good relationship with their lead regulator is vital to organizational success, and so it is inevitable that the design of internal risk management systems will reflect, at least in terms of the core elements, the risk evaluation process adopted by the regulator. The case study demonstrates the strength of these linkages in relation to RBS.

The third pillar of Basel II is market discipline. This reflects the view of the Basel Committee that *regulatory transparency* in relation to risk management and capital adequacy is vital to the success of the regulatory framework. The recent banking crisis has led to increased questioning about the adequacy of current levels of disclosure and calls for greater transparency. In particular, the accounting disclosures tend to be more limited than the regulatory ones, resulting in what has been termed a 'risk information gap' (Woods, 2007). It is too early to tell whether IFRS 7 disclosures will reduce this information gap, as the standard only became effective in January 2007.

Regulatory disclosure rules mean that banks must incorporate controls over reporting into their risk management systems, in order to ensure compliance. In summary, therefore, all three pillars of Basel II act as drivers of risk management within banks:

- *Pillar 1* encourages risk management thinking to focus on the three main areas of credit, market and operational risk.
- *Pillar 2* defines the features of the risk management system that will be monitored by local regulators.
- *Pillar 3* encourages risk transparency only within predefined guidelines.

Innovations in financial instruments

Over the course of the last 15 years, the derivatives markets have expanded rapidly, as institutions have sought new ways to hedge risks and increase profits. The growth has been aided by the development of new products, particularly in the credit derivatives market, with the creation of, for example, credit default swaps, collateralized debt obligations, credit linked notes and credit default swaptions. For example, International Swaps and Derivatives Association (ISDA) statistics show that the total year end value of outstanding credit default swap contracts rose from US$918 billion in 2001 to US$38,560 billion in 2008, representing a phenomenal rate of growth.

As Gillian Tett observes in her book *Fools' Gold* (Tett, 2009), the rush into derivatives was fuelled by the pressure on banks to search for ways of increasing the yield on their assets. If interest rates are low, assets in the form of loans will earn poor rates of return, but credit derivatives provide the scope to leverage up those returns, albeit by potentially taking on more risk. The need to manage the risks that may arise from trading large volumes of derivatives led to the development, by staff at JP Morgan, of the concept of Value at Risk or VaR. In simple terms, VaR is a summary measure of financial risk, and can be defined as the maximum likely loss on a portfolio over a specified holding period. For example, a bank might say that the VaR on its trading portfolio is $40 million, where the confidence level is 99 per cent and the holding period is the next trading day. This means that the bank expects that over the next trading day there is a 99 per cent chance that it will either make a profit or it will make a loss no bigger than $20 million.

VaR is a good example of how the risk management systems within banks generally have been influenced by regulation. VaR was originally developed for internal reporting use within JP Morgan but has since been incorporated into the banking regulations for use in determining capital requirements in relation to a bank's trading activities (market risk) and also for external risk reporting. Consequently, the growth of the derivatives market led quantitative risk specialists to devise a risk measure that is now used by banks around the world.[5]

Summary

All businesses have an incentive to manage their risks in order to avoid the threat of bankruptcy, but the preceding analysis clearly indicates that banks also face a number of other external pressures which have influenced the development of their risk management systems. The nature of bank balance sheets and stock market demands for higher returns on equity encouraged banks to increase their involvement in derivatives trading, whilst simultaneously finding a way to manage such risks. Contemporaneously, further pressure to manage risks came from regulation – either bank-specific or general governance regulations. As a result, there is a high level of standardization in the risk categories defined by banks and the primary structures used to manage those risks. The problem comes in how to manage the conflicting pressures: for safety from regulators versus profit from shareholders. The differing responses of financial institutions are revealed in the variation in approaches found in the risk reporting lines, level of granularity of analysis, the status of the risk function within the organization, and the extent to which risk exposure is reviewed in terms of judgements and not just mathematical models.

Overview of the risk management approach in the Royal Bank of Scotland

The role of the risk management function

In 2004 RBS managers were starting to respond to the challenge of working out the right model for a group of its scale, complexity and ambition – to add value as well as maintaining control. In 2004, a total of approximately 2,000 staff were employed within the risk management function at RBS out of a total group staff of 115,000. By 2006 the number of staff had increased to 4,250 serving a total group staff of 142,000. Proportionally, therefore, the function expanded over this period in terms of staff numbers.

The Head of Group Risk saw the role of Group Risk Management as being at the centre of what he described as a 'three lines of defence' model, still applicable in 2008. This is illustrated in Figure 5.2.

The first line of defence is provided by the managers within each business, who both own and are responsible for the day-to-day management of risks in their area. The risk controls and processes used for monitoring are designed and over-seen by the second line of defence – group risk management (GRM) and the broader 'risk community' that can be found across all of the divisions. They hold responsibility for creating the risk management frameworks and making sure they are being operated effectively. Consequently, part of the role of the business managers is to monitor controls and ensure compliance with group policies and methodologies. The third line of defence is internal audit, which is responsible for testing the adequacy and effectiveness of the controls within each area of business. Internal audit is thus entirely independent of GRM and its staff are not

1st Line of defence	2nd Line of defence	3rd Line of defence
The Business	Operational Risk	Group Internal Audit
Accountable for the ownership and day-to-day management and control of operational risk. Responsible for implementing processes in compliance with group policies. Responsible for testing key controls and monitoring compliance with group policies.	Responsible for the implementation and maintenance of the operational risk framework, tools and methodologies. Responsible for oversight and challenge on the adequacy of the risk and control processes operating in the business.	Responsible for providing independent assurance on the design, adequacy and effectiveness of the group's system of internal controls.

Figure 5.2 The three lines of defence model

Source: Annual Report, 2008, p. 118

seen as part of the risk management community. It was noted that the Internal Audit team would be the smallest part of the triangle.

The three lines of defence require a point of reference in terms of how much risk is acceptable, and this is provided via the specification of a risk appetite.

Risk appetite

The annual reports for RBS state that the Group Board of Directors sets the overall risk appetite and philosophy and that all directors participate in discussing strategy, performance and the financial and risk management of the company. In all companies, however, and in HBOS and RBS in particular, questions have been raised about the extent to which individual CEOs may dominate decision-making and the non-executive directors are able/willing to offer an opposing viewpoint. There is therefore some merit in investors exercising a healthy degree of cynicism about the statements on risk management structures that appear in annual reports.

Risk appetite in RBS is expressed in terms of residual risk – that remaining after controls have been put in place – and measured in both quantitative and qualitative terms. Customer perception is an example of a qualitative measure because 'happy customers are the life blood, so if you've got no happy customers you don't tend to have a happy business'. At a strategic level, therefore, new product launches will not just be risk assessed against, for example, the regulatory requirements such as the FSA's initiatives on treating customers fairly, but also the impact on the customer – what does the customer actually think of this?

Risk appetite in quantitative terms is measured or expressed at group level in terms of impact upon profit before tax, balance sheet strength and liquidity. In RBS, risk appetite was understood to be about how much they were prepared to lose in terms of provisions and write-offs, which is all part of the profit target. But they didn't have hard limits that say 'no more deals on that'. Losing more than a certain amount of money in a given period would not just damage the finances but also require the bank to go back to the market and declare it. Risk appetite is therefore expressed in terms of an arbitrary level of, say, 10 per cent of gross profit. Risks that, if crystallized, may cause such losses are classed as amber. Below that level they are green, and above they become red. All high-level risks are termed Priority One and are owned by a member of the Group Executive Management Committee.

Given that RBS operates a number of different businesses or divisions, the risk appetite in terms of acceptable losses varies across the range of activities and the respective levels are overseen by the Risk Committee (see below).

Overall objectives of group risk management

In RBS risk management was seen as just good husbandry to drive the business forward. Risk management is essentially about performance improvement. The view is that risk management plays four distinct roles:

- Adviser.
- Enforcer.
- Enabler.
- Ambassador.

In the *advisory* role, the function is involved in advising the executive board on the broad policies and processes required to effectively manage all material risks across the group. Advice on defining the risk appetite is also part of the remit, together with advice on policies for the monitoring of risk exposures against the declared risk appetite and compliance with the policies.

Enforcement requires the risk management function to establish a structure through which it is possible to ensure compliance with policies and procedures across the group. The structure will be discussed in more depth later in the case study, but in summary, the central function of GRM is relatively small with risk specialist units distributed out across all of the divisions. Divisions are defined in operational rather than legal terms e.g. Global banking and markets; UK retail and commercial banking; RBS insurance, etc.

The *enabler* role means that the risk function owns a set of core processes which are applied group-wide to control risks. Examples might be the credit approval processes, the VaR model that is used to measure market risk exposure, or the notifiable event process which ensures a rapid response to events which may threaten the financial or customer reputation of the bank. Ultimately, the aim is to enable front line businesses to be able to meet customer needs within an agreed framework of risk tolerance – the risk appetite.

The *ambassador* role involves taking the risk message out to other parts of the group, seeking to cascade the case for control across all of the divisions worldwide. In line with political diplomacy, this requires the establishment of mechanisms to ensure consistency in the message and this is nurtured through the development of what RBS term 'a risk community'.

Figure 5.3 Risk governance at group level

Source: Annual Report, 2008, p. 78

Governance structure

RBS's group strategy and risk appetite are set by the Board of Directors and implemented by the Group Executive Management Committee with additional support from a number of committees. The skeleton of the top level governance framework is illustrated in Figure 5.3 and each of the committees has a specific risk related role to play within the RBS group. With the exception of the Audit Committee and Advances Committee, all of the core risk management committees are executive committees that sit below Board level. This is not unusual but it raises questions about the level of influence over Board decisions that is exercised by the senior staff in the group risk function. They can advise, but no more.

Figure 5.3 also shows the Group Risk Committee and Group Asset and Liability Management Committee (GALCO) on the same organizational level. The Head of Group Risk – now renamed Group Chief Risk Officer – is a member of both committees which have complementary remits. The risk committee deals with the core processes used to control risks across the group, and the monitoring to ensure that risks are kept within the approved risk appetite. GALCO is more focused on capital management and control of group balance sheet risks. More detail on the stated roles and membership of the respective committees is given in Table 5.2.

Risk categories

As indicated in the section of external influences upon risk management in banking, the Basel regulations split bank risk into distinct categories for the purposes of calculating capital adequacy requirements. The categories are credit, market and operational risk.

Within RBS, as in other banks, these three risk categories are all significant. That said, they are not the only risks that are encountered, and so the risk

Table 5.2 Committees supporting the group board

Committee	Focus	Membership
Group Audit Committee (GAC)	Financial reporting and the application of accounting policies as part of the internal control and risk assessment process. GAC monitors the identification, evaluation and management of all significant risks throughout the group.	Independent non-executive directors
Advances Committee (AC)	Deals with transactions that exceed the Group Credit Committee's delegated authority and large exposures.	Members of GEMC Group Chief Credit Officer
Group Executive Management Committee (GEMC)	Ensures implementation of strategy consistent with risk appetite.	Business and function heads, as determined by the Group Chief Executive/Board
Executive Risk Forum (ERF)	Acts on all strategic risk and control matters across the group including, but not limited to, credit risk, market risk, operational risk, compliance and regulatory risk, enterprise risk, treasury and liquidity risk, reputational risk, insurance risk and country risk.	Group Chief Executive Group Finance Director Group Chief Risk Officer Chairman, Regional Markets Chief Executive, RBS UK Chief Executive, Global Banking and Markets
Group Risk Committee (GRC)	Recommends limits and approves processes and policies to ensure the effective management of all material risks across the group.	Group Chief Risk Officer Group head of each risk type Group Treasurer Chief Executive and Chief Risk Officer from each division Group General Counsel and Group Secretary, Group Chief Economist
Group Credit Committee (GCC)	Approves credit proposals under the authority delegated to the committee by the Board and/or the Advances Committee.	Members as determined by GEMC
Group Asset and Liability Management Committee (GALCO)	Identifies, manages and controls the group balance sheet risks.	Group Finance Director Chairman/Chief Executive from each division Group Treasurer Group Chief Risk Officer Heads of group functions
Group Chief Executive's Advisory Group (GCEAG)	Acts as a forum for the provision of information and advice to the Group Chief Executive. Forms part of the control process of the Group.	Group Chief Executive Group Finance Director Chairman and Chief Executives from each division Group Chief Risk Officer Group General Counsel and Group Secretary Group Directors, Strategy, Communications and Human Resources

categories are extended and change over time in response to developments both within the business and also the external environment. This is most clearly seen in comparing the key risks identified by the bank in 2004 versus those identified in 2006.

The starting point for risk categorization is corporate objectives and strategy, or how the bank makes money, and these are used to identify what might be called business risks. In 2004 there were two main ways:

- By traditional banking and lending money – credit risk.
- By trading and also operating exposure to movements in market prices such as interest or exchange rates – market risk.

By 2006, this had been extended to three sources of profit, as the bank's insurance arm (primarily a European-based operation) was becoming increasingly important within the group. In 2004, insurance premium income (excluding reinsurance) represented 36 per cent of the group's non-interest income, but by 2006 this had increased to 40 per cent. Presumably in recognition of this, insurance risk was added to the core categories.

- RBS insurance (Direct Line, Churchill, Privilege, Green Flag) – insurance or underwriting risk.

The three business risks are all managed through designated procedures which are commonly supported by extensive analytics and quantitative risk modelling.

Another risk category that was added between 2004 and 2006 was balance sheet liquidity. This was not a new risk, as it had always been managed through the Treasury function, but adding it to the list of core categories raised its profile group-wide. In practical terms, this meant that liquidity risk could be made, measured and monitored at divisional and business levels rather than simply being held 'at the top'.

Across all of its areas of business the bank encounters what it terms *enterprise risk*, which has both internal and external components. The internal risks refer to the risk of failure, omission or error in relation to people, processes, systems or assets across the organization. This is often known as *operational risk*. A simple example might be the omission of an element of training for a new member of staff, which results in them executing a process incorrectly, resulting in losses. The biggest category of internal risk is that resulting from human error, but inappropriate process design, failure to manage change properly and incomplete processing are also significant. The aim was to have no down time, no systems failing, and a zero tolerance of any failure across any activity on operations. At a basic level: every time you go to your ATM there is always money in it. Although this becomes articulated into certain degrees of tolerance, the aim is zero failure.

External risks arise because of threats from the external environment rather than from within, and may include business and political risks. Examples might

Box 5.2 Regulatory risk: example

The UK's Office of Fair Trading is conducting a study into the personal current account market and the fairness of the charges on such accounts. The OFT issued a report on its initial findings in July 2008 in which it found the position to be unsatisfactory, with the charging systems being opaque and complex. It is still consulting banks and consumers to find a solution.

Consequently, the group cannot reliably estimate the impact of any adverse outcome of the OFT's market study or investigation upon it, if any.

include fraud or money laundering activities, or computer hackers accessing the bank's systems. Reputational risk also falls into this category. The difficulty with external risks is that they are, to some extent, at arms' length and so harder to control. For example, reputational risk involves ensuring that RBS does nothing as a group that is not in line with their ethical and business philosophy, but measuring this can be tricky. One measure might be the number of hits against RBS in the press, but as a multi-branded group these figures may be higher than for a single branded bank such as Barclays. Interpretation of such a result is thus not straightforward.

The final risk category used by RBS is regulatory risk. This is expressed in terms of both risks and opportunities – i.e. managing both the risk of non-compliance and of failing to take advantage of the regulatory environment within the jurisdiction in which the bank operates. As a global organization, over the period 2003–8 RBS operated in around eighty different regulatory regimes and so ensuring full compliance is a major task. Regulatory risk is not just about compliance, however, it is also about changes in regulation and the broader implications they may have for the group.

At one level, the changes may arise out of an investigation by a regulator into a specific aspect of banking activity that is general to the sector (Box 5.2). Alternatively, regulatory risk can arise because of very specific and detailed changes in regulation, such as Basel II. Basel II has created much greater regulatory risk for RBS but has also had positive effects on its risk management processes. Establishing the additional data and analytic systems required to run Basel II required the, albeit temporary, creation of a new risk category – Basel II – which was project managed to ensure that all Basel II compliant systems were in place and functioning effectively by the required deadline. Even at the most basic level, getting to grips with the broader implications of such a change for a large global group is complex. In the six years leading up to Basel II, the Basel Committee on Banking Supervision published 147 papers, including three major consultations.

In implementing the new capital adequacy requirements for operational risk under Basel II, RBS wanted to apply what is termed in the regulation the Advanced Measurement Approach (AMA). Under this approach, each firm calculates it own capital requirements, by developing and applying its own internal risk measurement system, and the system must be validated by the FSA before it will be allowed to take advantage of the AMA. The AMA requires detailed types of scenario testing, and so the requisite data and systems needed to be put in place. Nonetheless, in terms of benefits, it was suggested that the Basel II project has driven much better relationship management ability and much better credit related data, allowing better management on a portfolio basis.

Table 5.3 Main risk categories in RBS

Risk type	Definition	Features
Credit risk (including country and political risks)	The risk arising from the possibility that the group will incur losses from the failure of customers to meet their financial obligations to the group.	Loss characteristics vary materially across portfolios. Significant correlation between losses and the macroeconomic environment. Concentration risk.
Funding and liquidity risk	The risk of losses through being unable to meet obligations as they fall due.	Potential to disrupt the business model and stop normal functions of the group. Significantly correlated with credit risk losses.
Market risk	The risk that the value of an asset or liability may change as a result of a change in market rates.	Potential for large material losses. Significantly correlated with equity risk and the macroeconomic environment.
Insurance risk	The risk of financial loss through fluctuations in the timing, frequency and/or severity of insured events, relative to the expectations at the time of underwriting.	Frequent small losses. Infrequent material losses.
Operational risk	The risk of financial loss or reputational impact resulting from fraud; human error; ineffective or inadequately designed processes or systems; improper behaviour; legal events; or from external events.	Generally immaterial losses.
Regulatory risk	The risks arising from regulatory changes/enforcement.	Risk of regulatory changes. Compliance with regulations. Potential for fines and/or restrictions in business activities.
Other risk	The risks arising from reputation and pension fund risk.	Additional regulation can be introduced as a result of other risk losses.

Table 5.3, from the 2008 annual report, summarizes the main risks faced by the group. The categories described are regarded as risk disciplines which need to be cascaded across the entire organization.

Horizon scanning

Whilst the main risk categories of credit, market and operational risks will persist over the longer term, the overall nature and scale of risks faced by an organization are not fixed. As already indicated, the risks evolve as the business evolves and developments in the external environment continually create new risks. Forty years ago the concepts of computer fraud or fraud through card skimming at ATMs would have been unknown, but now they rank high on the risk management priorities of financial institutions.

In order to prepare for new risks, RBS engages in what is commonly called horizon scanning. The group uses the term 'upstream risks' for a process which involves identifying what potential legislative, macroeconomic, social and regulatory events are occurring at about one, three and five years out in time. The logic is that if the potential risks can be identified, then they can also be evaluated in terms of their impact – positive or negative – and a mitigation plan put in place. The mitigation accelerates it, changes it, or if at all possible kills it dead. This anticipation of risks allows for influence of what is going to happen but also gives much more of a lead time to set up the implementation process.

In some respects, the risk forecasting process may be easier for highly regulated institutions such as banks, because so much of their risk is related to changes in regulation. In RBS, one example of a future risk that was being managed in anticipation (in 2006) was the European Union's Markets in Financial Instruments Directive (MiFID), which extends the coverage of the current Investment Services Directive regime to cover commodity derivatives, credit derivatives and financial contracts for differences (CFDs). MiFID was originally due to come into effect in 2006 but was delayed until late 2007 to give firms time to establish the systems needed for compliance. The directive impacts upon all institutions involved in trading financial instruments and means that investment banks such as RBS face additional requirements in relation to their internal organization of such deals – such as system control, investment advice, record keeping, etc. – and the transaction reporting processes. MiFID requires additional investment in systems because of the need for financial institutions to adhere to a code of best execution, taking into account price, venue, cost and speed, and to demonstrate transparency by retaining concise details of every trade for a period of five years.

Given the significance of MiFID to the global operations within RBS, responsibility for managing the risk was given to a senior manager. Both the upstream, or preparatory risk, and the downstream risk of ongoing compliance rests with the Chief Executive of Global Markets. In a similar vein, other major regulatory initiatives are also owned by senior management. For example, the SOX compliance is owned by the Finance Director. In practice, all key risks are owned by either the divisional CEO or, at a group level, by the relevant director reporting to the group CEO.

Risk ownership, operating oversight and reporting lines

Underlying principles

In the previous section Figure 5.3 identified the main committees at group level which play a role in risk management, but one of the biggest challenges for a Chief Risk Officer is to establish a structure by which risks can be cascaded down throughout an organization into the hands of the operational managers. This requires the specification of risk reporting lines within both the operational side of the business and also the risk management function itself. In RBS this form of infrastructure links the management of risks within divisions to the much bigger picture of overall group risk.

The group view is that risk management forms part of the day-to-day role of all members of staff, and they are assisted in this process by the following specialist functional staff:

- Risk management at both Group Risk and Divisional Risk levels: help with credit, market, operational, regulatory, enterprise and insurance risks. Will also help with providing quantitative risk analysis and analytics.
- Group Treasury: assistance with balance sheet, liquidity, funding and capital risks as well as hedging processes.

Both of these support functions are independent of the revenue generating businesses.

Internal audit supports the risk management process at group level by providing an independent assessment of the design, adequacy and effectiveness of internal controls. The Head of Internal Audit and Chief Risk Officer both report directly to the Audit Committee and the Group Chief Executive.

All members of the Audit Committee are independent non-executive directors. The Committee holds at least five meetings each year and in relation to risk management it is responsible for:

- Reviewing accounting and financial reporting and regulatory compliance.
- Reviewing the Group's systems of internal control.
- Monitoring the Group's processes for internal audit, risk management and external audit.

The effectiveness of group internal audit is reviewed externally every three to five years – currently by KPMG (former auditors of NatWest) – and there is an internal review overseen by the Audit Committee in the intervening years. KPMG's most recent review in 2007 concluded that the function operated effectively.

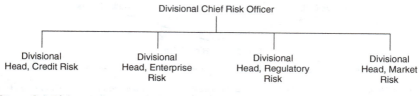

Figure 5.4 Risk management at divisional level

Operational responsibility for risk management

Responsibility for the implementation of group strategies rests with the Group Executive Management Committee (GEMC), the members of which are drawn from all of the group's key divisions and support functions. For example, the CEO of the UK Personal Banking division is a member of the GEMC and he/she owns the responsibility for risk within that division. A divisional Chief Risk Officer supports the process and oversees the implementation of the relevant risk policies and processes that have been established at group level. The divisional chief risk officer reports, in operational terms to the divisional CEO and in functional terms to the Group Chief Risk Officer.

Figure 5.4 shows that the core risk categories of credit, market, enterprise and regulatory are recognized across all the divisions of the group, although their significance will clearly vary widely from business to business. The additional risk categories, insurance and liquidity may also have divisional heads depending upon their level of importance in any given context.

Over the period 2005–8 the above structure was complemented by the formation of divisional audit committees responsible for reviewing each division's business. During 2008, the divisional audit committee structure was revised to take account of the acquisition of ABN AMRO, the significant international growth of the Group's businesses and best practice requirements. Details of this restructuring are not, however, available to the author. The divisional audit committees report to the Audit Committee.

The infrastructure described above underpins the independence of the operational and risk support functions, whilst also ensuring that group level messages are filtered down to divisions in a common and coherent way. It was also noted in the interviews that managerial responsibility for risk management was reinforced by risk ownership being built into performance management assessments, so that if there were significant operational failures in a division, a CEO is held responsible.

Reporting lines within the risk management function

Not surprisingly, the core risk categories or disciplines form the basis for lines of responsibility within the risk management function. Consequently, the Group

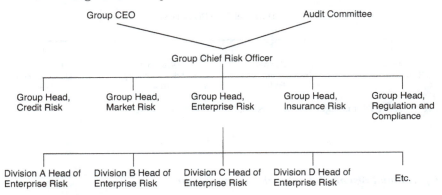

Figure 5.5 Risk function reporting lines

Chief Risk Officer is responsible for the work of Group Risk Officers covering each of the main categories. It was not made clear in the interviews, but this seems to imply that these group heads are the line managers for each of the relevant divisional heads as shown in Figure 5.5. The reporting lines for liquidity risk are also unclear, except insofar it is overseen by GALCO. Figure 5.5 is, therefore, based on informed guesswork. It is also clear that the management structure at senior level in RBS has undergone major reform over the last 18 months, and so any diagrammatic representations of reporting lines may change with the new staff in position. How the role of Executive Risk Forum fits in this structure is also unclear.

Additional support structures

The formalized structures outlined above reflect a view that risk is very much a support function that serves a clear purpose at both group and divisional levels. This was described in terms of a move towards what is known as the 'risk community'. At the head of this community is the Group Risk Committee which is made up of the following members:

> Group Risk Board = Group Chief Risk Officer
> + Risk discipline Heads e.g. Group Head of Credit Risk
> + Divisional Chief Risk Officers

The Board takes decisions on the strategic direction of the risk function within the group and on issues which impact upon more than one division.

Sitting beneath the risk board is the Risk Leadership Forum which includes around the top 150 people in terms of risk leadership rather than organizational status. The forum is not a formal organizational structure, but a way of 'spreading the word' about risk by the way that people operate. The forum members are listed in a Risk Leadership Directory which is updated yearly. They attend a number of events throughout the year and they play not only an ambassadorial role but also a risk leadership role across the group. Shared learning is part of the philosophy in the forum and one of the ways that this is done is by granting access to a library of books about risk and then asking members to condense the extensive content into about ten pages of real value. The summaries are then posted on the intranet.

At the time of the last interviews there were plans in place to complement the leadership forum with a Risk Academy designed to provide graduate trainees with an externally accredited Masters degree in risk. The aim was for the qualification to be accredited by the IFS and Chartered Institute of Bankers in Scotland. Such a scheme would allow graduates to see risk as a professional career that is a clear alternative to others such as accounting. As risk management becomes increasingly important, the recognition that it has professional standing is expected to increase. Unfortunately, it is not known to what extent these ambitions came to fruition as the main interviewee has now left RBS.

Conclusion: the group-wide impact of the risk management structure

CIMA's official terminology (CIMA, 2005, p. 53) defines risk management as the 'process of understanding and managing the risks that the entity is inevitably subject to in attempting to achieve its corporate objectives'. Applying this definition, it makes sense to evaluate the impact of the risk management structures within RBS in terms of group performance, but in the last three years this has been abysmal.

The approach to risk management described above evolved over the period following the acquisition of NatWest, but between 2000 and 2009 there has only been one period of stability in terms of the person holding the post of Group Chief Risk Officer. In 2000, the post was held by William Martin and in 2001 he was awarded the title of Risk Manager of the Year by the Global Association of Risk Professionals (GARP). The award cited Martin as spearheading four initiatives: group credit risk, group market risk, group operational risk, risk-adjusted portfolio analysis and economic capital, and the group risk management committee. These were seen as helping to ignite a 55 per cent jump in its share price over the course of the year 2000. Clearly, GARP hold the view that risk management has the potential to be a value adding function.

In January 2002 Richard Gossage, a former Director of Risk at NatWest, took over from Martin and stayed in post until January 2007. During this period, he developed the framework created by Martin but left the group shortly before the near-fatal ABN AMRO take-over. He was replaced by Peter Nathaniel, previously the Head of Group Risk at Citigroup, but Nathaniel resigned in June 2009 following the appointment of Nathan Bostock as Head of Restructuring and Risk. Presumably, Nathaniel found it difficult to see how two people could do what is effectively one job.

The lack of stability post 2007 clearly cannot be helpful in ensuring that risk management and internal control remains high profile and highly effective within RBS. Combined with the complexities of the need to recapitalize the group, the position over 2007–9 has thus been extremely difficult. Nonetheless, the roots of the ABN AMRO crisis may well be connected to the risk management structure put in place over the preceding decade.

Silo-based management

A key characteristic of the risk management structure within RBS, which is common across many banks because of the format of banking regulations, is the division of risks into specific silos, each of which is managed independently. Credit risk is distinct from market risk and operational risk, etc. Tools for measuring and monitoring each category of risk are well established and filter down across all of the divisions, as depicted in Figures 5.3–5.5, but this approach carries with it the danger of creating a narrow mind set. For example, it can lead to a complacent view that if all the core risk measures are indicating that a division is operating within safe limits, then there is no need to worry. The trouble is, at both divisional and group levels, risks can interact, creating a portfolio type exposure. What is more, the risks may be either positively or negatively correlated and so total risk is not simply the sum of all the individual ones. To assess the extent of *aggregate* risk exposure at group level is a massive challenge.

Possibly because of the complexity of some of the financial risks, and the sophisticated models that were needed to measure and monitor them, attention seems to have focused on the risks themselves rather than the underlying businesses. The divisional CEOs in RBS were receiving reports from heads of each of the respective risk disciplines and these were also being reported up to group level. At the same time, however, each CEO faced challenging returns on equity targets that impacted upon his/her remuneration. How does the CEO match ROE targets to the risks being taken except in terms of each separate silo?

The answer is far from clear for all banks and not just for RBS. As Anderson & Associates note in their report on risk management and corporate governance (OECD, 2009, p. 32) 'at the moment there is no single recognized way for organizations to link high level aggregate risks to low level transactional risks'. Finding the solution to this problem is like the holy grail of risk management.

The role of 'quants' in risk management

The problem of aggregating all of the risks within RBS is the task of the Chief Risk Officer, but if no mechanisms yet exist that enable this to be done, then a next best solution is sought. Despite the fact that not all risks can be quantified, the dominant fashion in financial services risk management over the last decade appears to have been that probability estimates rule, so risk management has been handed over to the 'quants' people. Credit rating mechanisms, combined with estimates of default probabilities, portfolio management and stress testing are all tools in common use to manage credit risk. These are complemented by the use of credit derivatives to more effectively manage the risks, but the pricing of such derivatives requires the use of ever more complex models. Similarly, market risk management is characterized by the use of Value at Risk models which, as already noted, are useful but have also been subject to widespread criticism. Scenario testing provides a useful complementary indication of possible levels of exposure. Even operational risk assessment has now been quantified, so that it is reported in terms of metrics of the percentage of operational risks falling into different categories such as external fraud, technology failure, process failure, etc.

Counting and measuring risks only gets you so far. It needs to be complemented by the application of thoughtful judgement about the implications of the figures and the cumulative impact of lots of different types of risk upon the overall organizational objectives. In the preface to his book (Rebonato, 2007) on why we need to manage financial risks differently, Ricardo Rebonato (who is interestingly, the Head of Quantitative Risk at RBS) uses the following quote from Karl Pearson (1889): '[T]here is considerable danger in applying the method of exact science to problems. ... of political economy'. (cited in Desrosieres, 1998) An obsessive focus on measuring risk can be both cumbersome and complex but not necessarily effective, as is so clearly demonstrated by the ongoing banking crisis.

The power – or lack of it – of risk managers

In her book about the demise of Bear Stearns (Kelly, 2009), Kate Kelly notes the lack of power exercised by risk managers at a strategic level 'Managers in places like risk management and operations were considered less important to the firm's core franchise and therefore largely excluded from important decisions.' All of the structures and formulae in the world are of limited use if the voices of those who understand them go unheeded, and the financial crisis has revealed a number of instances of the advice of risk managers being ignored.

For example, press reports on the collapse of Lehmann Brothers noted the 2007 departure of Michael Gelband as global head of the fixed income division after he railed against the bank's purchase of a collection of sub-prime mortgage lenders. The former *Financial Times* editor who became Lehman's head of communications in London is quoted as saying

> 'it was quite hard to stand in the way. That's not to say they didn't have proper risk management processes in place: they had some very good people doing it ... There was risk management but the prevailing atmosphere was for fast growth and special fast track treatment for what we now know were toxic deals'
>
> (Mathiason *et al.*, 2009).

In similar vein, press comment (Tett, 2009) suggests that RBS was also guilty of ignoring cautionary comment from risk staff. Ron den Braber was working at

RBS in London in 2003 when he became worried that the bank's models were underestimating exposure to credit risk. When his bosses failed to listen to his message, he left the bank. His explanation was 'group think' and a lack of understanding of how the models worked.

As this case study has shown, it is common practice for senior risk managers to be ranked one tier below board level. If the final say on strategic decisions rests with board members then it would seem to be advisable to promote the Chief Risk Officer to executive director level, to ensure a voice of caution is heard to the full.

The ultimate conclusion is that systems and structures are only one element of the risk management framework. People, the exercise of judgement and thoughtful consideration of aggregate rather than individual risk exposures all form other parts of the mix.

References

BIS (2005) 'Basel II: International convergence of capital measurement and capital standards: a revised framework', November, http://www.bis.org/publ/bcbs107.htm

CIMA (2005) *Official Terminology*, CIMA Publishing/Elsevier, Oxford.

Committee of Sponsoring Organizations of the Treadway Commission (COSO) (2004) *Enterprise Risk Management*, AICPA, New York.

Desrosieres, A. (1998) *The Politics of Large Numbers: A History of Statistical Reasoning* (Cambridge, MA: Harvard University Press).

FRC (2005) *Internal Control: Revised Guidance for Directors on the Combined Code*, Financial Reporting Council, London.

FSA (2003) *The Firm Risk Assessment Framework*, February, Financial Services Authority, London.

FSA (2006) *The Firm Risk Assessment Framework*, August, Financial Services Authority, London.

FSA (2007) *Our Pillar II Assessment Framework*, May, Financial Services Authority, London.

Hull, J. (2007) *Risk Management and Financial Institutions*, Pearson, Upper Saddle River.

ICAEW (1999) *Internal Control: Guidance for Directors on the Combined Code* (Turnbull Report), Institute of Chartered Accountants in England and Wales, London.

Kelly, K. (2009) *Street Fighters: The Last 72 Hours of Bear Stearns, the Toughest Firm on Wall Street*, Portfolio Hardcover, USA.

Mathiason, N., Connon, H. and Wachman, R. (2009) 'Banking's big question: why didn't anyone stop them?' *Observer*, 15 February.

OECD (2009) *Risk Management and Corporate Governance*, Richard Anderson & Associates, Kingscliff, NSW.

Rebonato, R. (2007) *Plight of the Fortune Tellers*, Princeton Unversity Press.

Tett, G. (2009) *Fools' Gold*, Little Brown, London.

Woods, M. (2007) 'Significant information gap that requires regulators' attention', *Financial Times*, 26 September.

Part III

Risk management in practice

The public sector

6 Case study

The Department of Culture, Media and Sport

> Risk management – getting the right balance between innovation and change, on the one hand, and avoidance of shocks and crises, on the other – is now central to the business of good government.
>
> (Tony Blair, November 2002)

Government exposure to risk

In common with private sector organizations, the UK government has become increasingly aware of its exposure to a wide range of risks, and the need to manage such exposures. The Treasury's Risk Support Team, which is currently responsible for the co-ordination of the risk management programme in central government, explicitly recognizes a growing need to ensure effective procedures are in place for handling risks at strategic, programme and operational levels.

Government departments provide a wide range of public services including healthcare, education, national defence, the payment of social benefits and support for business. Each of these services involves exposure to some level of risk, and the risk scenarios faced by government are further complicated by the growing practice of contracting with partner organizations for the delivery of services and projects. Given this broad and varied context, there is a need for a mix of both generic and contextually specific guidelines on risk management.

This case study explains how these guidelines have been developed over recent years, and how they are now used within a single government department – the Department for Culture, Media and Sport (DCMS) – to assist in ensuring the achievement of departmental strategic and operational objectives. The case study does not seek to reach a judgement about the quality of risk management within government, but merely to describe current practice, and highlight relevant issues.

Historical background

The decision to integrate risk management into the generic management control system within UK government can be traced back to a recognition that best practice developments in corporate governance within the private sector could be usefully adapted and applied to the public sector. The adaptation and adoption of private sector management practices into the public sector is broadly termed New Public Management and its underlying thinking reflects the shift towards a more neo-liberalist approach to government since the 1980s.

Private sector thinking on governance first began to impact upon government thinking in relation to risk management with the publication of best practice guidance on internal control in the Cadbury Report (Cadbury Code, 1992). The code served as a background to the drafting of a 1994 Treasury guidance note on risk management, that was later supplemented by the so called 'Green Book' (HM Treasury, 1997 and 1999) which required government organizations to take account of risks and uncertainties in evaluating the costs and benefits of public projects. In October 1999, following the publication of the Turnbull Report (ICAEW, 1999) on private sector governance and internal control, a Modernizing Government Action Plan was announced which would incorporate initiatives to improve the management of risk within central government.

A National Audit Office (NAO, 2000) report from that time clearly highlights the influence of private sector thinking upon risk management in the public sector. The report declared that:

> Work is under way on the appropriate method of adapting the principles of the Turnbull Report to the central government sector. A key element of this work is the drive to have strategic risk identification and management processes in place in all government organizations, encompassing the whole range of risks relating to objectives which organizations face.
>
> (NAO, 2000, p. 39)

Reflecting this position, the modernizing government action plan required all departments to prepare (by September 2000) documents outlining the framework of procedures to be used in ensuring the incorporation of risk into decision-making.

In February 2000 the Treasury hosted a seminar on risk management which brought together speakers from the public and private sector. In addition, a paper (Hood and Rothstein, 2000) was commissioned from two eminent LSE academics to report on the potential benefits and pitfalls of adapting private sector risk management practices to public sector use. At the same time, the NAO, in conjunction with PricewaterhouseCoopers, carried out a survey (February 2000) of 257 departments, agencies and non-departmental public bodies (NDPBs) in order to better understand existing risk management practices. The survey, which had a 92 per cent response rate, asked about their understanding of risk management and its importance to their performance, how they identify and assess risks, and the action they take to deal with them. The survey results were complemented by interviews with 12 departments and two focus groups with representatives from departments. In summary the results indicated that whilst the vast majority of departments understood the importance of risk to the achievement of their objectives, their understanding of how to manage the risks affecting service delivery was much less clear. More worryingly, 38 per cent of departments did not routinely assess risks, although a small majority did have procedures for reporting risks to senior management.

Perhaps partly in response to the survey findings, and the recognition that not all government organizations had basic risk management processes in place, the Treasury then published a first draft of *Management of Risk: A Strategic Overview* (HM Treasury, 2001) which has since become known as the Orange Book. The publication offered a basic introduction to the concept of risk management and the resources and processes needed to implement it within government organizations.[1]

In July 2001 a Strategy Unit (part of the Cabinet Office) study on risk and uncertainty was announced, and its report, *Risk: Improving Government's Capability to Handle Risk and Uncertainty* was published in late 2002 (Cabinet Office, 2002). The outcome was a two-year programme based around the principles laid down in the NAO (2000) report, aimed at appointing departmental risk improvement managers and stimulating improvements in risk management across all central government departments. The so-called Risk Improvement programme, tied in to the 2004 Spending Review, was overseen by a Treasury-based Risk Support team, reporting to the Ministerial Committee on Public Services and Public Expenditure, and the Prime Minister. The programme was closely monitored at the highest levels of government, and generated two reports to the Prime Minister (May and December 2003), an interim report to the Chief Secretary to the Treasury (July 2004) and a final report to the Prime Minister in December 2004.

One of the interesting features of the risk programme reports was the inclusion of examples of Best Practice in risk management from a range of sources, including the private sector – BP, AstraZeneca, Zurich and others – as well as the best local authorities and organizations from Canada, Australia and New Zealand. Given that the programme's emphasis was on *improvement* these examples provided benchmarks against which departmental managers could evaluate their own performance. More fundamentally, the second report recognized that improvement could only be evaluated via a formal risk assessment framework,[2] which was to be used by departments to help them judge, on a common basis, their risk management capabilities and how far these were helping them to achieve their objectives. The framework, described as 'a tool for departments', was, and still is, used by nearly all main departments to assess five aspects of their capabilities:

- Leadership.
- Risk strategy and policies.
- People (skills, etc.).
- Partnerships.
- Processes.

Capability is evaluated in terms of two measures of results or effectiveness:

- The quality of risk handling.
- The impact of risk management on achieving departmental outcomes.

The self-assessment process for risk management will be discussed in greater depth later in this case study, but at this stage it is worth noting the government intentions which underpinned its creation. The framework identifies these as follows:

- To give managers a broader overview of the department's risk capabilities and risk management effectiveness.
- Monitoring and review of the effectiveness of internal controls to support the Statement of Internal Control. (See below for details of this.)
- Reviewing/reporting on risk management capability and impact on performance and outcomes.
- Identification of areas of good/poor performance and establishment of priorities for action.
- Aiding in peer reviews and benchmarking, both internally and externally.

On a five-point scale, at the time of the risk programme's second report in December 2003, most departments classed themselves at either level two or level three in terms of risk capability i.e. either implementing, or had already implemented the necessary risk management arrangements. However, very few felt they had fully embedded their risk management into departmental operations (level 4) and none placed themselves in the highest category. Furthermore, there was significant variation across departments, with smaller ones tending to score more highly than the larger ones. By implication, there was still progress to be made.

The final report to the Prime Minister (HM Treasury, 2004, p. 2), in October 2004 concluded that 'government has improved its ability to handle risk over the past two to four years, and is continuing to do so'. This view was supported by a separate NAO study but the future outlook was rather more cautious, suggesting that:

> while significant progress has been made by departments to improve their risk management, they have further to go to demonstrate that they have made effective risk management a central part of their day-to-day general management processes in a way that can fully deliver improved performance and other benefits. They need to continue to develop their ability to take risks and innovate, to keep projects and programmes on track, to handle complex service delivery networks, and to be ready with the means to respond to the fast-moving and unexpected turn of events … Good progress has been made – but the key is now to maintain the momentum.
>
> (NAO, 2004, p. 6)

The Risk Programme ended in December 2004 and since then the basic tools and structures for risk management within government departments and Non-Departmental Government Bodies (NDGBs) have remained largely unchanged. A number of additional guidelines have been published, particularly in response to often well publicized failures of risk management such as the loss of personal data by HM Revenue and Customs in autumn 2007, when disks containing the National Insurance details of up to 25 million British adults went missing. The event triggered a subsequent Cabinet Office investigation into data handling by the government. The resulting reports (see Cabinet Office, 2007; Coleman Report, 2008) concluded that departments needed to sharpen their information risk management procedures and be held more accountable for related failures via the introduction of a requirement to include information assurance issues in their annual report. In addition, a number of documents have been updated to reflect new thinking, but the onus of responsibility has passed to departmental management for the implementation of the recommendations that emerged from the Risk Programme. These include the appointment of a Risk Improvement Manager tasked with the job of establishing risk management processes and internal controls, using the risk management assessment framework to monitor progress, and evaluating success in terms of improved delivery of public services.

In working to improve their risk management processes, departments are currently able to draw upon a range of resources for assistance and guidance, including the risk support team at the Treasury, the Strategy Unit, the Civil Contingencies Secretariat, and the Office of Government Commerce.[3] In addition, the Public Sector Benchmarking Service (PSBS) hosts a database of examples of good practice in risk management. Now that the Risk Programme is complete, the database is only available for archival use, but during 2002–4 the PSBS was also used to facilitate networking and the sharing of good practice in risk management across government. This was done by granting public sector employees access to discussion groups, knowledge banks, electronic documents, notice boards, links and a helpdesk/enquiry service. The scope for learning and performance improvement from such knowledge sharing is huge and is continued today via a number of external support groups for public sector risk managers. Examples include the Association of Local Authority Risk Managers (ALARM) and the Central Government Special Interest Group within the Institute for Risk Management, both of which organize regular conferences and local meetings to share ideas, problems and best practice.

Generic versus domain-specific approaches to public sector risk management

One of the characteristic features of the UK government's approach to risk management is the extensive amount of generic material that is core to the risk programme across all of central government. The issue of balancing generic guidance with departmentally specific approaches to risk management is therefore worthy of some debate, particularly given the comment made almost ten years ago by Hood and Rothstein (2000) that 'risk management systems in government tend to be policy-domain-specific' (para. 1.1, p. 1).

Hood and Rothstein's observation was underpinned by a belief that, despite the fact that the risks facing government departments and public bodies are often identical to those faced by private sector businesses – e.g. litigation; IT failure; fraud; reputational damage or financial risks – the organizational framework of the public sector is fundamentally different. In organizational terms, a great deal of government service delivery involves activities which are shared across departments and other public bodies. For example, the Change4Life campaign, launched in September 2008 by the Department of Health, is aimed at reducing levels of childhood obesity by 'bringing together a coalition of health and education professionals, the third sector, community groups, industry and the media with the shared aims of improving children's diets and levels of activity so reducing the threat to their future health' (Department of Health, 2008). The campaign targets are shared by the Department of Health, the Department for Children Schools and Families and the DCMS, and the additional involvement of community and third sector groups means that risk management for this type of project is a big challenge. For example, how is responsibility for risk shared out between the different parties? Where does responsibility for internal control design rest? If parties to a policy are legally independent, then how can the authority of one over another be effectively exercised? These questions have no simple, uniform answers.

Cross-cutting activities, requiring the co-operation of multiple agencies, are now commonplace in both central and local government and they pose the following specific challenges for risk management:

- A danger that systems designed to reduce risk will simply lead to blame being shifted between member organizations, whilst failing to focus on the need to create public value. The end result may then be that the politically weakest, rather than the best equipped bodies may end up carrying the responsibility for particular risks.
- A danger that mechanistic approaches to risk management will encourage a tick box, procedural mentality in which there is little intelligent and reflective consideration of risk exposures. The tendency may be to protect the organization rather than provide the public service, thereby undermining the role of public organizations as the risk bearers of last resort.
- In the absence of strong levels of trust across the linked organizations, the transparency of risk exposures and control systems may be undermined.

Extending the idea of linked risks even further, government is also concerned with what is commonly termed systemic risk, which can cause the domino like collapse of linked organizations. The recent banking crisis was characterized by the risk that if one big institution fell, then it could bring many more down with it, causing a massive threat to the overall banking system and broader economy. Such system-wide risks can only be managed at government level.

The significance of multi agency arrangements for public service delivery, and the threat of systemic risk exposure together imply a need for risk management systems in government which can cross organizational boundaries, whilst retaining a consistency of approach. In other words, there is a strong, prima facie case, for central government to provide generic guidelines that can be used across a wide range of public bodies.

The case in support of generic risk management guidelines is countered by arguments focusing on the diverse nature and scale of the risk exposures faced by different parts of the public sector. In terms of operational detail this is clearly true: the consequences of IT systems failure in the military defence arena may be much more significant than in the context of, say, public libraries. That said, both national defence and libraries are both public services aimed at providing public 'value', and so risk can be defined in terms of the threats to the provision of those services.

The issue of whether risks are domain specific – to a particular organization or government department – or generic in nature – is resolved in practice by a two-tier system of risk management which blends the generic with the more specific 'local' knowledge. Central government departments such as the Treasury, Strategy Unit, and OGC provide generic documentary guidance to all public bodies, and establish certain rules on external risk reporting. These guidelines are then reworked – to a greater or lesser degree – by the risk managers within individual departments or public bodies – to make them applicable to their own particular risk appetites and profiles. Table 6.1 details the type of generic and locally

Table 6.1 Current sources of risk management guidance in central government, 2009

Generic guidance	Localized guidance (example)
Treasury	*DCMS*
• Orange Book (2004) • Risk Assessment Framework (2004; updated 2009) • Statement of Internal Control pro-forma (DAO (Gen.) 09/03; Chapter 21, Government accounting)	• Risk Management Guide • Risk Management Policy Statement • Risk registers • Risk assessment in submissions to Ministers and management board
Office of Government Commerce	
• Guidelines on Business Continuity Management (2001) • Managing Risk with Delivery Partners (2005)	
Project-focused guidance	
• Risk Management Strategy: see http://www.ogc.gov.uk/documentation_and_templates_risk_management_strategy_.asp • Risk Management Framework: see http://www.ogc.gov.uk/documentation_and_templates_risk_management_framework_.asp	
Online support tools	
• Public Sector Benchmarking Service (archive only) – best practice database • Cross-government internet and intranet sites offering guidance, good practice and other resources	

specific guidance that is currently available in central government, with the two categories of information working to complement one another.

Consistency across government is retained, *up to a point*, by all risk managers being involved in applying a common self-assessment procedure to their own risk management processes (as described earlier), the outcome of which is monitored by the National Audit Office. The net result is a balancing act between generic and specific internal controls, which is largely managed via the application of rules on transparency, designed to ensure that risk management failures are not just recognized internally but identified in the department's annual report. The details of how this works in practice are covered in greater depth later in this case study.

In order to best understand how these guidelines are applied in practice, it is helpful to place them into a departmental context. The next section therefore profiles the DCMS before looking in depth at the practice of risk management within that department.

Profile of the Department of Culture, Media and Sport

Overview

The principal activity of the DCMS is to take responsibility for the setting and implementation of government policy on a wide range of cultural and leisure activities.

More specifically, its primary responsibilities range across:

- The arts.
- Sport.
- National Lottery.
- Tourism, libraries, museums and galleries and the historic environment.
- Broadcasting and the creative industries such as film and music.
- Press freedom and regulation.
- Licensing and gambling.
- 2012 Olympic Games and Paralympic Games.

The department's other diverse responsibilities include:

- Listing of historic buildings and ancient monuments.
- Management of the government art collection and the royal parks.
- Provision of humanitarian assistance in the event of a disaster, e.g. 2005 London Tube bombings.

The DCMS also holds lead policy responsibility for 54 public sector bodies that fall outside the departmental accounting boundary, but help to deliver the department's strategic aims and objectives. Over 95 per cent of the department's expenditure is channelled through these bodies, which receive grants-in-aid that are governed by funding agreements which identify what each body will deliver in return for the public funding allocated to it. The public sector bodies for which DCMS is responsible include:

- Three public corporations e.g. Channel 4 Television Corporation.
- Two public broadcasting authorities, including the BBC.
- Museums and galleries, e.g. British Museum, Tate Gallery.
- British Library.
- Arts Council of England.
- English Heritage.
- Design Council.
- Sport England.
- Olympic Delivery Authority.
- National Lottery Commission.

The range and scale of operations covered by the department and its associated public bodies are usefully illustrated by some key statistics, highlighted in Box 6.1. The statistics also indicate the extent to which the department must engage and work closely with other agencies in pursuit of its objectives.

The economic sectors for which DCMS is responsible account for nearly 10 per cent of the economy (Civil Service, 2009). Despite this, in operational terms the DCMS is one of the smallest government departments, with approximately 470 staff in post during the year to July 2009 (excluding the associated NDPBs and Royal Parks). The departmental resource budget, which covers annually managed expenditure was £2,906 million for 2008–9, and the capital

---

Box 6.1 Key statistics

- The British Museum received over 6 million visits in the year to March 2008.
- The nine royal parks have 37 million visitors per year.
- Since its inception in 1994 the National Lottery has raised over £23 billion for good causes.
- Over 279 million visits were made to public libraries in 2008.
- £950 million was taken at cinema box offices in 2008, and British films accounted for 31 per cent of the takings.
- Over 4,000 people are working for contractors on the Olympic Park and 9 per cent were previously unemployed.
- The DCMS is responsible for maintaining the list of over 500,000 listed buildings in England.

The Arts Council's Own Art scheme has 250 galleries across the UK participating in an interest free loan scheme to encourage the purchase of new art.

employed was £4,659 million, although £4,510 million of this was in the non-departmental public bodies. The story underlying these figures is that the DCMS is effectively 'a small government department with an almost wholly strategic function, where policy development, industry sponsorship and stewardship of the sponsored bodies form the core functions, with a small number of staff in support dealing with accommodation, HR, finance, etc.' (DCMS, 2009).

Governance structure

The DCMS was restructured in 2008 and is now organized into four directorates, two covering policy and programmes and two covering management of the corporate centre.

The Department's policy and programmes are delivered by:

- The Government Olympic Executive, which holds responsibility for the delivery of the 2012 Olympic and Paralympic Games.
- The Partnerships and Programmes Directorate. This is made up of three small sector teams – culture, media, and sport and leisure – and the Evidence and Analysis Unit, which manages departmental research and supports the development of evidence-based policy.

The directorates that form the corporate centre are:

- External Relations.
- Corporate Services.

The Department is managed by a Board led by the Permanent Secretary, who is answerable to parliament for departmental expenditure. The remaining Board members are:

- Director General, Government Olympic Executive.
- Director General, Partnerships and Programmes.
- Director, Finance.
- Director, Corporate Services.
- Director, Legal Services.
- Director, External Affairs.
- Four non-executive directors.[4]

The Board is supported by an Executive Committee, Audit Committee and external Advisory Board. The Audit Committee meets quarterly, and its members are drawn from a mix of other central government departments and the private sector.

Political guidance and oversight of the DCMS are the responsibility of the Secretary of State for Culture, Media and Sport, who is assisted by three other Ministers with sector responsibilities, namely the Minister for Sport, Minister for

Culture and Tourism and a Minister for Creative Industries. In addition, a Minister for the Olympics oversees the Department's work in preparation for the Games, although she currently works out of the Cabinet Office. The senior management structure of the Department is illustrated in Figure 6.1.

The annual financial statements of the DCMS and the many public bodies which it sponsors are subject to annual audit by the National Audit Office (NAO). In addition, the NAO conducts regular value for money reviews of activities within the culture, media and leisure sectors including, for example, the preparations for the London 2012 Olympic and Paralympic Games and the government's preparations for digital switchover. Oversight of the NAO is carried out by the sixteen-member cross-party Public Accounts Committee (PAC) and the DCMS Annual Report 2009 contains an Annex detailing its progress in responding to PAC recommendations arising from the value for money reviews.

The annual report also contains a Statement on Internal Control (SIC), the origins of which can be traced back to the Turnbull Report (ICAEW, 1999).[5] The SIC provides an assurance that the control systems underpinning all activities within the department are effective. A key implicit element in providing such assurance is the requirement to formalize risk management processes and conduct regular risk assessments and reviews of risk management processes.

The requirement for formalized risk management structures as a prerequisite for completing the SIC is well illustrated by the short extract from the most recent DCMS report given in Box 6.2. The Review of Effectiveness which is contained in the extract, is required under the pro forma for SICs that is published by HM Treasury, and its requirement to affirm the effectiveness (or otherwise) of the internal control system is actually more onerous than the private sector equivalent under Turnbull. Directors of listed companies are merely required to state that they have undertaken a review of internal controls, but do not have to confirm effectiveness or state the results of the review's findings.

The SIC in Box 6.2 is extracted from the 2009 annual report and accounts of the DCMS, and it provides a useful summary of the core elements of the internal control and governance system within DCMS – the Board, Executive Committee, Audit Committee and Internal Audit Services. The next section deals in depth with how the risk management framework operates within the Department.

Risk framework within the DCMS

What is risk?

The DCMS uses the Cabinet Office Strategy Unit (Cabinet Office, 2002) definition of risk:

> We define risk as 'uncertainty of outcome, whether positive opportunity or negative threat, of actions or events. It is the combination of likelihood and impact, including perceived importance'.

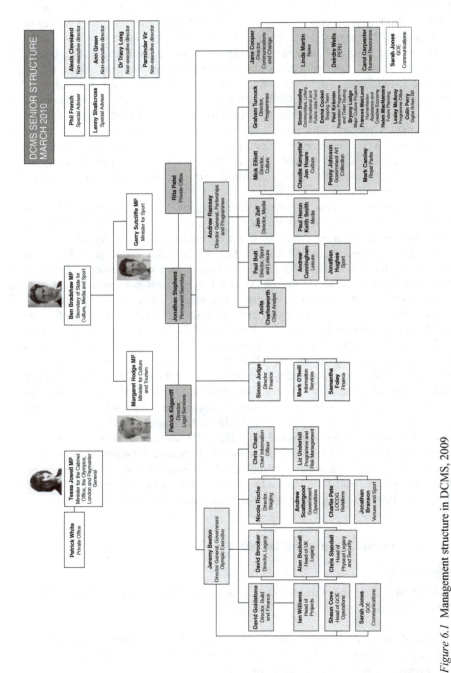

Figure 6.1 Management structure in DCMS, 2009

Source: http://www.culture.gov.uk/images/publications/dcms_structure-organisationalchart.pdf

Box 6.2 Review of effectiveness (extract from the SIC of the DCMS, 2009)

As Accounting Officer I have responsibility for reviewing the effectiveness of the system of internal control. My review of the effectiveness of the system of internal control is informed by the work of the internal auditors and the executive managers within the Department who have responsibility for the development and maintenance of the internal control framework, and comments made by the external auditors in their management letter and other reports. I have been advised on the implications of the result of my review of the effectiveness of the system of internal control by the Audit Committee, and a plan to address weaknesses and ensure continuous improvement of the system is in place.

The key elements of the system of internal control are set out above and contribute to my review of the system's effectiveness. The following governance bodies also inform my view:

- The *DCMS Board*, which meets regularly to set the Department's long term strategy, direction and priorities. At present the Board comprises me, the Directors General, four Directors and four non-executive members (there were three non-executive members during 2008–09).
- The *Executive Committee* allocates resources for delivering departmental priorities. It is the mechanism for accountability on programme delivery and core departmental business. It comprises the executive members of the Board plus DCMS's Directors.
- The *Audit Committee* meets four times a year and supports me in my responsibilities for risk management, control and governance. The chairman sits on the Board, which takes decisions based on the advice received. At present, the Audit Committee comprises a non-executive chairman and five other non-executive members (there were three non-executive members during 2008–09). Others in attendance include the Finance Director, National Audit Office Directors and the Head of Internal Audit.
- *Internal Audit Services* (IAS) operates to Government Internal Audit Standards, and is provided by Communities and Local Government. IAS submits regular reports, which include the Head of Internal Audit's independent opinion on the adequacy and effectiveness of the arrangements for risk management, control and governance, together with actions for improvement, as agreed with management. For the year ended 31 March 2009, that opinion concluded that there were no significant control issues arising that require disclosure in this Statement.

Notwithstanding that opinion, I am conscious that last year saw considerable organisational change within the Department. That made it particularly important to ensure that the design and operation of internal controls still met the needs of the Department. I am satisfied that has been the case. However, I continue to attach importance to embedding our new risk management framework, to ensuring that the assurance process is improved and so to increasing the overall reliability of our internal controls.

(DCMS Annual Report, 2009)

Basic risk management framework

Building on the definition of risk given above, the Risk Management Policy Guidance for the Department states that the risk management framework describes 'the culture, processes and structures directed towards the effective management of potential opportunities and threats to the Department achieving its objectives'. The guide depicts the risk management framework, illustrated in Figure 6.2, as a cycle which begins with the setting of clear objectives, and ends with a review and report on risk management which feeds back into the cycle of risk identification, assessment and specification of risk responses. The declared aim is for all staff to develop the necessary skills and experience to be able to work through the main steps of the risk management framework.

The cycle appears to be a modified version of the risk management process (Figure 6.3) that was developed by the Institute of Risk Management and published in their risk management standard.

(Institute of Risk Management, 2002)

Risk identification

The most common types of risk that could face DCMS are shown in Table 6.2 grouped under three core headings – external, operational and change. The risks identified in the table are drawn from the Orange Book and provide a basic, generic starting point for staff to use in developing an organizational risk profile. In its guidance to staff on how to begin identifying risk, the Orange Book splits the process into two stages:

- *Initial risk identification* where risks have never before been identified in a structured way, or a new activity or project is planned.
- *Continuous risk identification* provides a structure for identifying new risks that may arise as a result, for example, of organizational change.

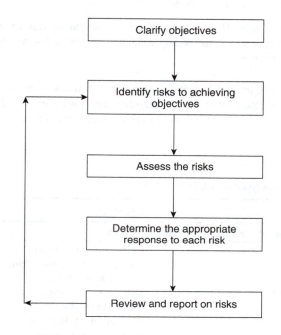

Figure 6.2 Risk management framework in DCMS

Source: DCMS, Risk Management Policy Statement and Guidance, July 2009

Figure 6.3 Core elements of the risk management process

Source: Adapted from Institute of Risk Management (2002)

The intention is that staff will be involved in continuous risk identification and horizon scanning in which upcoming risks are recognized and anticipated. Risk identification incorporates:

- A definition of the risk that includes both the cause and the consequence.
- Acknowledgement of potential interdependencies between different types of risk, e.g. poor management of cash resources creating problems for staff recruitment.

Table 6.2 Common types of risk facing DCMS

Risk category	Example
1 *External:* not wholly within the department's control	
1.1 Political	Change of government
1.2 Economic	Staff recruitment and retention; global economic conditions
1.3 Socio-cultural	Demographic change
1.4 Technological	Systems obsolescence
1.5 Legal	EU legislation/directives
1.6 Environmental	Waste disposal; climate change
2 *Operational:* related to current operations – delivery, capacity and capability	
2.1 Delivery	
2.1.1 Service/product failure	Failure to deliver within agreed terms
2.1.2 Project delivery	Failure to deliver on time/budget
2.1.3 Capability and capacity	
2.1.4 Resources	Poor budget management; insufficient HR capacity/skills; loss of assets e.g. via fraud or theft
2.1.5 Relationships	Lack of clarification of partner roles; poor customer satisfaction levels
2.1.6 Operations	Overall capacity to deliver
2.1.7 Reputation	Lack of confidence or trust
2.2 Risk management performance and capability	
2.2.1 Governance	Compliance with requirements
2.2.2 Scanning	Failure to identify threats/opportunities
2.2.3 Resilience	IT system capacity to withstand attack
2.2.4 Security	Of physical assets
3 *Change:* created by decisions to pursue objectives beyond current capability	
3.1 PSA targets	New and challenging targets
3.2 Change programmes	Programmes that threaten capacity to deliver
3.3 New projects	Investment decisions; project prioritization
3.4 New policies	Expectations create uncertainty about delivery

- Identification of specific action(s) that could be taken to address the risk.
- Assignment of the risk to an owner who takes responsibility (and has sufficient authority) for its monitoring and management.

In revising its risk management systems in 2009 the DCMS extended its risk identification analysis by creating four core risk categories – strategic, programme and project risks, business and joint (partnership) risks. This reconfiguration aligns more closely with a new way of working in the department which leans towards programme and project management.

Risk assessment

After risks have been identified, they are grouped and ranked according to the likelihood of their occurrence and their expected impact. For this purpose, the DCMS uses a 3 × 3 matrix that estimates the impact and likelihood of the risks *from a departmental perspective*. This latter point is important for two reasons. First, the risk management process is built around departmental not divisional objectives. Second, the level of risk from a divisional or project perspective may be higher (or lower) than from a departmental viewpoint, particularly where risks are shared.

Likelihood/impact matrices are commonly used by risk managers. The exact design of the matrices will vary from organization to organization but the underlying principle remains identical: the aim is to be able to classify risks in terms of the two dimensions. The DCMS has three classes of both impact and likelihood. These are high, medium and low. Tables 6.3 and 6.4 detail the definitions applicable to each of these classifications.

At this stage in the process, the risks being classified are the inherent risks i.e. those which may occur assuming no management controls are in place to reduce their likelihood or impact. It is also acknowledged that the assessment may rely simply on a 'gut reaction' although where possible it is desirable to support this with evidence from past experience, records or expert advice.

The combined impact and likelihood estimates are then drawn together to create a 3 × 3 matrix which indicates the overall assessment of inherent risk, as shown in Figure 6.4. The matrix shows the level of inherent risk scored on a scale of 1 to 9, with 1 being the highest and 9 the lowest. The classification into the high/medium/low zones directly reflects the perceived severity of impact upon service objectives if the risk crystallizes, and this is reflected in the subsequent level of control and frequency of monitoring.

Level 1 risks are both high impact and high likelihood, and thus classed as extreme. These risks and the related controls are automatically escalated up to the next level in the organizational hierarchy. The term 'high' is applied to the risks scored 1 to 4, and for all such risks the Department requires that a contingency plan be prepared, detailing how to manage the situation if the risk materializes. The plan allocates responsibility for monitoring of the risk to a different

Table 6.3 Impact

Classification	Definition
High	• Serious impact on costs (over £1 million), output, and ability to meet objectives • Medium- to long-term effect and expensive to recover • Serious impact on departmental reputation
Medium	• Significant waste of resources – over £100,000 • Impact on operational efficiency • Medium term impact, expensive to recover • Adverse impact on departmental reputation
Low	• Minimal/minor loss, delay or interruption • Easily and quickly remedied • Little or no effect on departmental reputation

Table 6.4 Likelihood

Classification	Frequency	Definition
High	Probable: more likely than not to occur	• Potential to occur within the next budget period • Has occurred recently
Medium	Possible: may occur at some time	• Is there a history of occurrence? • External influences may make it difficult to control
Low	Remote	• Has not occurred • Unlikely to occur

individual from the risk owner, who must regularly report the status of the indicators, and ensure regular reviews of the contingency plan.

The estimated inherent risk i.e. before any action is taken to manage it – is compared to the departmental risk appetite in order to assess the action required. If the risk is significantly higher than the tolerable level, then an appropriate and proportionate control needs to be identified. If it is lower than tolerable, then it raises the question of whether it is currently over controlled. For example, there is a low risk appetite in respect of all projects that are critical to the departmental mission, and so any such projects that have a high inherent risk score (1–4) will require a control(s) or other response to reduce this down to a tolerable level.

The Departmental risk appetite, or willingness to tolerate risk, therefore influences the nature and extent of controls that will be applied to mitigate a risk, but it is not generic across all risk types. The DCMS risk appetite is established via

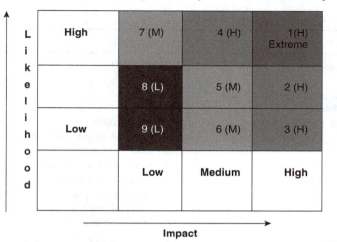

Figure 6.4 Inherent risk matrix

discussion and collective action amongst the Heads of Divisions, Project Directors, Board members and the Permanent Secretary.

The Risk Management Guide identifies seven primary groups of risk for the DCMS and the risk appetite for each is shown in Table 6.5. This list serves as a guideline only, but clearly reflects sensitivity to those risks which may threaten the fundamental operations of the Department.

The residual risk – that which remains after controls are in place – is then compared to the risk appetite. The comparison facilitates assessment of the effectiveness of controls, because if the inherent and residual risks are very similar, then the controls are having minimal impact. The DCMS refers to the comparison of residual risk to risk appetite as a RAG (red, amber, green) assessment:

- *Red*. The control(s) are not in place or will not reduce the risk to an acceptable level.
- *Amber*. The control(s) is insufficient to reduce risk to the tolerable level, or is not yet in place but is expected.
- *Green*. The control(s) is in place and working effectively to reduce the risk to a tolerable level.

All of the departmental, divisional or project risk registers include a column to indicate the risk's status under the RAG assessment, and an explanatory narrative to justify the rating.

Once identified, prioritized, and given a RAG status, all risks are then managed through acceptance, reduction, transfer or avoidance. With selected controls in place, individuals are assigned ownership of the risk and take responsibility for

Table 6.5 Primary risk groups within DCMS

Risk type	Risk appetite
Reputational	Medium to low
External	Medium
Regularity, propriety, finance and accountability	Low
People and internal systems	High to medium
Delivery	Low on PSA targets and major/critical projects
	Medium on other activities
Policy/project risks	Linked to project type:
	• Speculative: high
	• Standard: medium
	• Mission critical: low
Partnership	Low – if linked to PSA targets or critical projects/functions

Source: Risk Management Guide, 2005

monitoring progress against the controls to ensure that the risk remains within tolerable levels and does not threaten the achievement of objectives. Feedback from the monitoring is then used to review and possibly modify both the objectives and the control process itself.

Risk monitoring

There are four key elements in the risk monitoring process within DCMS: individual ownership of risks, maintenance and updating of risk registers, internal audit/risk reviews, and the end of year risk self-assessment.

Risk ownership is only of any value if the responsibility is accompanied by the power to take necessary action. Staff guidance also encourages owners to embed risk reviews into standard management processes such as divisional meetings and one-to-one meetings, so that risk management does not simply translate into another layer of bureaucracy. The philosophy is one of trying to get everyone involved in recognizing that risk is part of their day job, and so the use of divisional 'risk champions' to promote risk management has purposefully been avoided. Perhaps inevitably, the net result is that the embedding of risk-based thinking consequently takes longer.

Risks are managed at three levels within the DCMS: the strategic level, programme level and project/operational level. These reflect the way in which strategic objectives are translated and cascaded down into operational decisions and activity within the Department and risk registers are maintained at all levels.

A generic format for the risk register applies across all three levels within the Department (see Table 6.6). The registers are subject to quarterly review, and the aim is for them to be interlinked, so that the major departmental objectives and associated risks are allocated down into divisions, projects and individual performance plans.

The strategic risk register contains around twelve risks, covering risks to the major objectives detailed in the corporate plan. Departmental strategic objectives are split into two categories. The first category covers its key priorities over the 2008–11 spending review period, all agreed with HM Treasury. These are as follows:

- Encourage more widespread enjoyment of culture, media and sport.
- Support talent and excellence in culture, media and sport.
- Maximize the economic impact of the Department's sectors.
- Deliver a successful Olympic Games and Paralympic Games with a sustainable legacy and get more children and young people taking part in high quality PE and sport.

The second category of strategic objectives are linked to the broader government aims and objectives laid down in the Public Service Agreements (PSAs) which set out the Government's highest priority outcomes for the period 2008–11. Each PSA has a lead Department, a number of contributing departments and a delivery agreement that sets out plans for achieving its targets and the role of key partners.[6] The DCMS is leading on one PSA – 'to deliver a successful Olympic and Paralympic Games with a sustainable legacy and get more children taking part in high quality PE and sport'. In addition, the Department has a specific role in the delivery of six other PSAs where the main delivery body is another government department.

The strategic risk register therefore includes risks such as those seen as threatening departmental funding, delivery of the Olympic project or the achievement of PSA targets. The register is reviewed quarterly by the Board and also discussed at the Audit Committee meetings. Strategic risks are also subject to review by internal audit, who report their findings back to both the risk owners and the Audit Committee.

The majority of strategic risks percolate down into the Divisional Risk registers, following the cascading down of the linked operational responsibility. This mapping of one register into another is, however, sometimes problematic and made more complex by the fact that many of the DCMS's strategic objectives require them to work with partners. Although a senior member of the department is named as the lead individual responsible for each strategic objective, it is recognized that a number of the strategic objectives require co-operation and the sharing of responsibility across a number of agencies. For example, the objectives of encouraging more widespread enjoyment of sport, media and culture and supporting talent and excellence in these fields both involve partnerships with

Table 6.6 DCMS risk register

Division/project/policy						Date	
Description of risk and what is at risk	Risk rating	Risk tolerance	Risk owner	Risk response, control and assurance	Gaps in control and assurance, including what action is being taken to close these gaps		RAG status
What is the risk category? Strategic Programme or project Operational Joint with delivery partner(s) What is the risk that will prevent us from achieving our objective? You should make clear what objective is at risk and this should be cross-referenced to our business plan.	Expressed in likelihood and impact	What is level of risk that you would be content with?	Individual with the authority to manage the risk	Controls in place to reduce the risks to achieving the objective. The person responsible for the controls. The process by which the risk owner is given assurance that the risks are sufficiently controlled. What action is being taken?	*Control.* Do the assurances identify that any of the controls are not working or are not fully implemented? *Assurance.* Are there controls where no assurance is available? What actions are planned to close gaps? Who is the person responsible for this and when do they need to be done by?		How content are you with the existing controls? *Green.* Totally content, no further action needed *Amber – green.* Content but we are taking more actions to increase contentment *Amber – red.* Not content, and we are taking action to increase contentment *Red.* Worried and don't know what to do

Source: DCMS Risk Management Policy Statement and Guidance, July 2009

Figure 6.5 Partners involved in DCMS strategic objective on culture, media and sport

NDPBs as well as other parties such as local authorities (under the terms of local area agreements[7]).

The huge problem of linking strategic risks to specific divisional and individual projects can usefully be illustrated by reference to the objective of encouraging more widespread enjoyment of sport, media and culture. The range of partners with whom the DCMS has to work in pursuit of this objective is illustrated in Figure 6.5. The partners are essential because, for example, the DCSF is responsible for child involvement in such activities, but the facilities are provided by sponsored bodies. In addition, local authorities, commonly tied in to regional networks, have themselves got target participation rates set as part of the local area agreements. The strategic objective is thus shared and so, therefore, are the risks. In order to manage Departmental performance against the objective, each partner group has an individual senior member of staff from the DCMS named as the lead, who carries responsibility for management of the associated partnership arrangements, including the risk management. Joint risk registers are also used to assist in clarifying lines of responsibility.

Working down through the Department, the divisional risk registers follow the common format and are also reviewed at least quarterly. Moving from division to the individual project or policy, the responsibility for risk also tracks the operational responsibility. In principle, therefore, all staff can see a route up through the Department, from their personal objectives and risk ownership back to the strategic objectives. Ensuring that this is the case in practice is, however, much more difficult.

A random sample of Directorate or Project risk registers are reviewed every six months by members of the Department's finance team.

Internal audit

Historically, the internal audit function operated from within DCMS but given the small scale of the department, the function itself was also only very small, employing just four people. A decision was therefore taken a few years ago to outsource the internal audit work to another, larger, central government department: Communities and Local Government. The DCMS staff moved across and the outsourced staff retained full access to the DCMS intranet, etc., but the bigger team now gives the Department access to more people with specialized skills, e.g. computer fraud, which were not previously available in-house. In essence, therefore, the outsourcing reduced risks for the DCMS by making it less susceptible to internal audit staffing problems and granting access to greater audit skills.

Internal audit adopts a risk-based approach to its work, reporting back to both the Audit Committee and the risk owner when control weaknesses are identified. Internal audit also reports to the Audit Committee on how well strategic risks are being managed, in addition to undertaking ongoing reviews of the wider internal control process across the Department.

Self-assessment

Internal audit provides an objective review of how well risks are being managed, but as already indicated, Treasury policy also requires all government departments to undertake an annual self-assessment of their risk management processes, in order to complete the SIC that is published in the annual report.

Guidelines on the framework to be used for the risk management assessment were first published by HM Treasury in 2004 and marginally updated in 2009. The framework is an adaptation of the EFQM Excellence Model and is based around seven core questions that can either be used centrally within a department or devolved for self-assessment by business units or partner organizations. In the case of the DCMS, the NDPBs now hold responsibility for conducting their own risk assessments.

In addition to offering a department some insights into the effectiveness of its risk management strategies, enabling any gaps to be readily identified, the self-assessment process encourages the development of clear risk guidelines for more general use. For example, the National Portrait Gallery has a web page: (http://www.npg.org.uk/visit/booking/schools-and-colleges/risk-assessment.php) which outlines the potential health and safety risks facing educational groups visiting the gallery, and how these risks may be minimized.

The seven top-level questions to be answered in preparing the self-assessment fall under three core headings covering capabilities, risk handling and outcomes. The questions are as follows:

Capabilities

- Leadership: do senior management and Ministers support and promote risk management?
- Are people equipped and supported to manage risk well?
- Is there a clear risk strategy and risk policies?
- Are there effective arrangements for managing risks with partners.

- Do the organization's processes incorporate effective risk management?

Risk handling

- Are risks handled well?

Outcomes

- Does risk management contribute to achieving outcomes?

These questions are supplemented by lower-level ones which explore each of the areas in more depth. For example, in terms of leadership, the subsidiary questions ask if the senior management take key risk decisions, support innovation and ensure clear accountability for risk management.

Performance in the assessment is measured on a five-point scale intended to enable a department to gauge its progress in improving its risk management capabilities and effectiveness.

Performance

Capability

Encompasses issues of leadership, policy and strategy, people, partnerships and resources and processes. In other words, are the elements in place in terms of leaders, guidance, staff and resources to grant the ability to manage risks effectively?

Performance in this category is measured as follows:

1 Awareness and understanding.
2 Implementation planned and in progress.
3 Implemented in all key areas.
4 Embedded and improving.
5 Excellent capability established.

Risk handling and outcome

This addresses the organization's ability to anticipate and manage strategic risks, undertake effective planning and target setting, and manage risks effectively so that objectives are successfully achieved. Performance in this category is measured as follows:

1 No evidence.
2 Satisfactory.
3 Good.
4 Very good.

5   Excellent.

The scale allows a department to monitor its overall progress over time, but also to benchmark its performance in terms of both types of activity (leadership, strategy, people, etc.) and across divisions or business units. Such monitoring also provides scope for benchmarking bilaterally or multilaterally across organizations.

In the section on historical background in this case study, it was noted that in December 2003 most government departments scored themselves around 2 or 3 on the self-assessment scales, indicating that risk management was being or had been implemented but was not embedded, and so there was scope for further progress. The ending of the risk programme and transfer of risk management responsibility to departments has helped to stimulate progress but there remain a number of key challenges.

The big challenge: the management of partnership risk

The cross-cutting strategies of central government pose particular challenges for departments such as DCMS which are tasked with pursuing strategic objectives which straddle multiple government departments as well as regional and local groups and NDPBs. Such partnership working can make risk management especially difficult, as already debated within this case study.

The extent of partnership working and the growth of arrangements such as public private partnerships for major construction projects has been rapid in the years since the Treasury Risk Programme ended in 2004, but the government has been supportive in developing some common guidelines for risk management under such circumstances (see, for example, the OGC's publication *Managing Risk with Delivery Partners*, 2005). The latter draws attention to the fact that even when some operational and financial risks are transferred to partner organizations, the overall delivery and reputational risks will generally be retained by the department. Under such circumstances the need to review internal risk management processes to accommodate shared risks is paramount.

The OGC identifies a number of core issues to consider in redrafting a risk management system to incorporate partner risks. These focus on such things as clarification of risks at pre-contract stage, obtaining assurance about the adequacy of partners' risk management systems, and ensuring that all inherent risks have been accounted for in the partnership agreement. Ultimately, however, if a department's accounting officer has to sign the SIC confirming the effectiveness of the internal control system then that officer will seek firm reassurance about partnership risks.

In the case of the DCMS, the responsibility for providing such assurance lies with the relevant heads of division and is managed as shown in Box 6.3. Such practice suggests that departments are learning about how to manage and control their exposure to partnership risk but simultaneously the landscape within which public services are delivered continues to increase in complexity. Under such

---

Box 6.3 Partnership risk assurance

Heads of Division are required to confirm in their assurance statements that where risk is transferred to a partner organization they understand the risk-management systems they have in place and that *key risks are identified in sponsored bodies' Funding Agreements* and covered in their out turn reports.

Guidance has been issued to Heads of Sponsor Divisions on the risk management aspects of working in partnership with NDPBs, including a *suggested list of questions* to ask on risk as part of the ongoing dialogue they should have with their sponsored bodies. This has highlighted the need for any NDPB risks which could have a material impact on the department's reputation, on the delivery of its strategic priorities or which might result in a call for extra resources to be *escalated to the department's management board.*

---

circumstances effective risk management has a premium value for departmental managers, and managing risks needs to be fully integrated into day-to-day management.

Update

Since this case study was completed, the DCMS has undergone a transformation of its working/delivery methods and has revised its risk management system accordingly. Some details of the revised approaches are available from the department's website (www.culture.gov.uk).

References

Cabinet Office (2002) *Risk: Improving Government's Capability to Handle Risk and Uncertainty*, Strategy Unit, London.

Cabinet Office (2007) *Data Handling Procedures in Government: Interim Progress Report*. Cabinet Office, London, December.

Cadbury Code (1992) *Report of the Committee on the Financial Aspects of Corporate Governance: The Code of Best Practice*, Professional Publishing, London.

Civil Service (2009) *Department for Culture, Media and Sport: Progress and Next Steps*, Civil Service Capability Reviews, London, March.

Coleman Report (2008) *Independent Review of Government Information Assurance*, Cabinet Office, London, March.

DCMS (2009) *Annual Report and Accounts 2009*, Stationery Office, London, July.

Department of Health (2008) 'Launch of Change4Life: a national movement to tackle childhood obesity' available at http://www.dh.gov.uk/prod_consum_dh/groups/dh_digitalassets/documents/digitalasset/dh_087867.pdf

EFQM (2002), *The Excellence Model*, European Foundation for Quality Management, Brussels.

Hood, C. and Rothstein, H. (2000) 'Business risk management in government: pitfalls and possibilities', Annex 2 in National Audit Office, *Report by the Comptroller and Auditor General. Supporting Innovation: Managing Risk in Government Departments*, Stationery Office, London, pp. 21–35.

HM Treasury (1997) *Guidance on Corporate Governance: Statements on the System of Internal Financial Control*, HM Treasury.

HM Treasury (1999) *Guidance on Corporate Governance: Statements on the System of Internal Financial Control*, HM Treasury.

HM Treasury (2001) *Management of Risk: A Strategic Overview*, HM Treasury.

Institute of Chartered Accountants in England and Wales (ICAEW) (1999) *Internal Control: Guidance for Directors on the Combined Code* (Turnbull Report), ICAEW, London.

HM Treasury (2004) *The Risk Programme: Improving Government's Risk Handling*. Final Report to the Prime Minister (December).

National Audit Office (NAO) (2000) *Report by the Comptroller and Auditor General: Supporting Innovation: Managing Risk in Government Departments*, Stationery Office, London.

7 Case study
Birmingham City Council

Risk and governance

Risk management is one element within a broader local government governance framework that was first developed jointly by CIPFA (Chartered Institute of Public Finance and Accountancy), SOLACE (Society of Local Authority Chief Executives) and the Local Government Association in 2001 (CIPFA, 2001). In 2007 this was updated and reissued by CIPFA, along with accompanying guidance notes (CIPFA, 2007). The framework is based on a belief that 'good governance structures enable an authority to pursue its vision effectively as well as underpinning that vision with mechanisms for control and management of risk' (CIPFA, 2009). In addition to guidance notes, the framework is supported by examples of best practice aimed at helping councils to review and, where necessary, redesign their own governance structures, regardless of the specific executive arrangements currently in operation.

The 2007 CIPFA framework identifies six core principles of good governance. These are adapted for local government use, but based upon the Good Governance Standard for Public Services (OPM/CIPFA, 2004). The principles define good governance as follows:

- Focusing on the purpose of the authority and on outcomes for the community and creating and implementing a vision for the local area.
- Members and officers working together to achieve a common purpose with clearly defined functions and roles.
- Promoting the values for the authority and demonstrating the values of good governance through upholding high standards of conduct and behaviour.
- Taking informed and transparent decisions which are subject to effective scrutiny and managing risk.
- Developing the capacity and capability of members and officers to be effective.
- Engaging with local people and other stakeholders to ensure robust public accountability.

In other words, risk management is core to good governance.

Historical background

In the UK, the development of governance standards that promote the development of robust risk management systems has been simultaneously accompanied by an evolution in the process of central government inspection and audit of local government performance. Detailed discussion of the history of Best Value, Comprehensive Performance Assessment and the current Comprehensive Area Assessment[1] falls outside the scope of this case study, but a brief review of the evolution of these systems is useful in putting local authority risk management into a broader context.

The 1999 Local Government Act introduced a duty for all councils, and other local government bodies to put in place arrangements to secure continuous improvement via a system known as Best Value. The Act also gave the Audit Commission general powers to inspect councils. Over the period 2000/1 the Audit Commission's inspections took the form of Best Value reviews of individual services within councils. Complementing the Best Value process, the Audit Commission also published a paper (Audit Commission, 2001) emphasizing the responsibility of both senior management and elected members to manage key strategic risks in local government and to develop formal risk management systems to assist this process. Most important, the Audit Commission also highlighted how risk management might be useful in the production and monitoring of the Best Value performance plans that formed a central plank of the government's agenda for local authority performance improvement.

In 2001, the conclusion was reached that a broader form of performance inspection was required, and Comprehensive Performance Assessment (CPA) was introduced in 2002. CPA took the form of an audit and inspection framework, described by the Audit Commission as drawing 'on a range of information such as performance indicators, assessments of corporate capacity, audit and inspection reports, and stakeholder opinions to reach a single judgement about the performance of a local body' (Audit Commission, 2006, p. 2). The framework for the CPA assessment varied according to the type of local government body being inspected, but for the period 2002–5 the net result was a CPA rating which classified a council as excellent, good, fair, weak or poor. The rating system was revised for 2005–8 with the introduction of a new methodology – the so called 'harder test' – which used a five-point star scoring mechanism on a scale ranging from zero to four stars.

Regardless of the detail of the rating system, the resulting CPA score was important to a council because it affected access to funding as well as their broader public reputation. In addition, CPA directly increased the pressure on councils to introduce formal risk management systems by incorporating risk assessment and management procedures into the CPA judgement.

The CPA assessment (Audit Commission, 2006a, b) includes a judgement on the extent to which risks and opportunities are incorporated into both strategic and operational decision-making. Audit Commission inspectors identify and evaluate evidence to enable them to assess the extent to which the internal control environment enables a council to manage its significant business risks. In order to obtain the highest possible score under CPA a council must demonstrate that risk management practices and assurance frameworks are fully embedded in the council's business processes and that these are overseen by an audit committee which is independent of the executive function, with terms of reference that are consistent with CIPFA's governance guidance. The standards are therefore demanding, and strongly mirror the recommendations for good private sector practice that are contained within the Turnbull Guidance on Internal Control.

The risk management assessment under CPA forms part of what the Audit Commission term the use of resources element of the performance inspection, and this is carried forward into the arrangements for Comprehensive Area Assessments which took effect in 2009. In summary, the CPA/CAA inspectors pursue what are termed key lines of enquiry (KLOE), in this case KLOE 2.4, to evaluate a local council's performance in the area of risk management. Full details of the content of KLOE 2.4 and the type of evidence sought by Audit Commission inspectors to support their judgement can be found on the Audit Commission's web site, but the inspection covers the following main areas:

- Basic structures for risk management – linking risks to strategic objectives; likelihood – impact analysis and ownership of risks.
- Embedding of risk management into core processes including policy making, planning and performance management.
- Counter fraud and corruption arrangements, including both proactive and reactive work, and the encouragement of a counter-fraud culture across the council.
- Systems of internal control and annual evaluation of internal control effectiveness; oversight by an Audit Committee.

The above brief history shows that between 2001 and 2009 there were significant developments in the evolution of risk management thinking in relation to UK local authorities, accompanied by both external guidance and also central government pressure to integrate risk into the performance management process. The strength of the link between performance and risk management is an issue which is central to the case study of Birmingham City Council, and it is a dimension of risk management systems that appears to be better developed within the public sector than within the private. Unusually, therefore, the case may offer lessons to be learnt by risk managers in both large and small private sector businesses.

Autonomy in the design of risk management systems

It is important to note that despite the CAA inspection system, or its predecessors, local authorities still have a significant level of autonomy in determining the way in which they establish systems to identify, assess, manage and respond to the entity's risks, and account to their stakeholders for their performance in this regard (Crawford and Stein, 2004; Audit Commission, 2001). There are plenty of points of reference for authorities to use in designing their risk management system, including the core standards such as that jointly drafted by the Association of Insurance and Risk Managers (AIRMIC), the Institute of Risk Management (IRM), and the Association of Local Authority Risk Managers (ALARM) (AIRMIC/IRM/ALARM, 2002), the COSO framework for Enterprise Risk Management (COSO, 2004) or the Australia Standard for Risk Management AS4360 (Standards Australia, 2004).

Local authority managers can also get help on risk matters by accessing guidance that is available from organizations such as ALARM, whose publications cover a wide range of relevant issues such as the management of fraud, partnership risks and the benchmarking of risk. ALARM also offers training programmes for both professional and academic risk management qualifications in addition to shorter seminars and workshops across the UK. Alternatively, help can be sought from the Improvement and Development Agency (IDEA), which encourages improvements in local authority service provision, and also runs the Beacon Scheme to encourage sharing of good practice.

It can therefore be seen that the risk management system within Birmingham City Council has developed within a context of autonomy of choice, but that autonomy needs to be viewed as constrained by existing thinking as expressed in the current risk and governance standards, and central government pressure to continually improve performance management.

Sources of data reported in the case study

The material used in the case study is drawn from a number of different sources, but primarily upon internal documentation from the city council and interview transcripts. In preparation for the interviews, publicly available information on the risk management system and practices was reviewed, in addition to internal documentation obtained from the internal audit department.

Extended interviews, attendance at management meetings and training sessions, and a guided walk through the software used to manage risks were all used to collect further evidence on both the risk management structure and also how it is used in practice. Interviewees included the Head of Internal Audit, other members of staff in Birmingham Audit, and the council's Chief Executive.

Corporate profile

The city

Birmingham is England's second city, covering 267.8 km^2 in the West Midlands conurbation and the city is the hub of the region's economy. The view of the Audit Commission inspectors is that 'the regional economy is driven by what happens in Birmingham and the Council's leadership role is critical to the prosperity and well being of the region' (Audit Commission, 2007, p. 10).

The local authority area covers a population of approximately 1 million, although 3 million live within the 'travel to work' area. Despite significant levels of inward investment in recent years, the region has suffered from substantial job losses within its former core industries of car manufacturing and vehicle components. Consequently, the economy has refocused and 80 per cent of jobs in the city are now in the service sector. Nonetheless, Birmingham's unemployment level of 7.6 per cent is significantly above the national average, and the highest within the Core Cities group[2] whilst incomes are below both the national and regional averages.

The population of Birmingham is characterized by its ethnic diversity, with almost 30 per cent coming from minority ethnic communities (primarily South Asian). There is also great diversity in the level of prosperity across the city, with both affluent suburbs but also poor housing estates where levels of unemployment are high and health poor. Overall, the levels of crime are better than in most large cities, but health and skill levels in the population are significantly worse than the national average. For example the life expectancy of men in Birmingham is 2.3 years less than the national average.

The council

Birmingham is England's largest local authority and also one of the largest in Europe. The metropolitan authority employs approximately 59,000 people and for the 2008–9 financial year its budget is estimated at £3,209 million. The council provides a wide range of services, but the major ones are education (including capital projects for schools), housing and a range of social services for adults, children and families. Other services include planning and building approval, the provision of leisure, sport and cultural facilities, and transport and highway maintenance projects. The vast majority of funding comes from central government, with only around a third of total income generated from local taxes, rental income and other sources. The key statistics in Box 7.1 give an overview of both the scale and range of services provided by the council. It is clear that behind these statistics lies a complex and large scale organization, which faces a wide range of risks that need to be carefully monitored and managed. To begin to understand how this is achieved in practice, we need to consider the governance model within which the provision of services is managed.

The governance model

The model of governance used by the authority is a leader and cabinet system. The cabinet is made up of ten senior full time members (councillors) plus the leader of the council, who acts as the chair. The Leader of the Council is required, by law, to publish and maintain a forward plan of the work of the Cabinet, and a copy of this is posted on the council's website.

Each cabinet member takes responsibility for a specific portfolio but all non-cabinet councillors can contribute to decision-making; elected members jointly

---

Box 7.1 Key statistics, 2008–9

- 173,846 pupils taught in 426 schools
- 13,044,240 school meals prepared by the in-house provider
- 64,097 Council houses maintained by the Council
- 5,897,472 visits to leisure facilities
- 4,485,832 visits to libraries
- 822,000 museum and art gallery attendances
- 2,675 hectares of parks maintained
- 475,000 tonnes of domestic waste collected
- 65,000 tonnes of trade waste collected
- 170,000 collections of bulky household waste
- 45,000 tonnes of recyclable paper waste collected
- 2,499 kilometres of road maintained
- 3,523,585 hours of home care provided
- 254,039 weeks of external residential care (adults and communities)
- 820,000 service responses dealt with at neighbourhood offices
- 7,800 planning applications handled

Source: Birmingham City Council, *Key Facts*

---

determine the pattern of spending and the priorities within the budget. The detail of both portfolio and ward level decisions are made public. The work of Cabinet is overseen by a total of eight overview and scrutiny committees, and responsibility for chairing the main scrutiny committees is shared between the different political parties.

In practical terms service provision is the joint responsibility of both politicians and executive staff. Consequently, the cabinet is complemented by officers of the council, headed by the Chief Executive. He/she is responsible for their own directorate and supported by a corporate management team (see Figure 7.1) made up of four strategic directors. The strategic directors head up the: (1) adults and communities, (2) children, young people and families, and (3) housing and constituencies directorates, and the fourth one, which includes development as well as leisure, sport and culture. In combination, the directorates cover the full range of services provided by Birmingham City Council. The Executive Management Team, comprising both Cabinet (portfolio holders) and strategic directors, meets once a week for policy review and development. This team is the local authority equivalent of a private sector Board of Directors.

Individual services fall under the remit of specific directorates. For example, in Birmingham the adults and communities directorate includes service areas encompassing provision of support for adults with mental health issues, support for carers looking after elderly, disabled or sick adults, provision of elderly residential care homes and day centres, and also adult education. Within the UK, the exact matching of services to directorates varies between different local

Corporate Management Team

```
                    ┌─────────────────────────────┐
                    │      CHIEF EXECUTIVE         │
                    │   (Head of Paid Service)     │
                    └─────────────────────────────┘

┌───────────────────────────┐     ┌───────────────────────────┐
│  STRATEGIC DIRECTOR OF     │     │        CORPORATE          │
│  ADULTS & COMMUNITIES      │     │  DIRECTOR OF GOVERNANCE   │
│                            │     │    (MONITORING OFFICER)   │
└───────────────────────────┘     └───────────────────────────┘

┌───────────────────────────┐     ┌───────────────────────────┐
│  STRATEGIC DIRECTOR OF     │     │  CORPORATE DIRECTOR OF    │
│  CHILDREN & YOUNG PEOPLE   │     │        RESOURCES          │
│                            │     │    (SECTION 151 OFFICER)  │
└───────────────────────────┘     └───────────────────────────┘

┌───────────────────────────┐     ┌───────────────────────────┐
│  ACTING STRATEGIC DIRECTOR │     │  CORPORATE DIRECTOR OF    │
│  OF DEVELOPMENT            │     │        CHANGE             │
│  ACTING STRATEGIC DIRECTOR │     └───────────────────────────┘
│  OF LEISURE, SPORT & CULTURE│    ┌───────────────────────────┐
└───────────────────────────┘     │  CORPORATE DIRECTOR OF    │
                                  │   HUMAN RESOURCES &       │
                                  │       EQUALITIES          │
┌───────────────────────────┐     └───────────────────────────┘
│  ACTING STRATEGIC DIRECTOR │     ┌───────────────────────────┐
│  OF HOUSING & CONSTITUENCIES│    │ ACTING DIRECTOR OF POLICY │
└───────────────────────────┘     │      & DELIVERY           │
                                  └───────────────────────────┘

                                  ┌───────────────────────────┐
                                  │  CORPORATE DIRECTOR OF    │
                                  │     PUBLIC AFFAIRS        │
                                  │   & COMMUNICATIONS        │
                                  └───────────────────────────┘
```

Figure 7.1 Management structure in Birmingham City Council

Source: Birmingham City Council (2009a)

authorities, but the overall governance structure remains very similar across the sector. Service directors report to their relevant strategic director, and also take responsibility for management of the operational staff.

Figure 7.1 also shows corporate directors who are directly answerable to the Chief Executive, and form part of the management team. These directors are responsible for key support functions such as finance, human resources and communications/public relations within the City council.[3]

One of the important characteristics of the governance structure in local authorities is the extent to which it requires interaction and good understanding between members and officers – the members make the policy decisions and the staff implement them. A good working relationship between the two groups is thus an essential prerequisite for effective service provision and budget management.

Risk management in Birmingham City Council

Motivation

The motivation to adopt risk management and introduce the associated formal control systems within Birmingham City Council can be explained as being a response to a number of different influences. First, is the influence of the various codes of governance which can be found within the public sector and most particularly those coming from CIPFA and SOLACE. The second impetus to adopt risk management has come from external audit, which takes the view that local authorities should have effective systems in place in order to manage risk. The third influence is a comprehensive performance assessment and the inclusion of risk management arrangements within the key lines of enquiry used in the use of resources assessment. It is also recognized that the comprehensive area assessment, which is now coming into operation, will place an even stronger emphasis on risk management.

Risk management strategy

As indicated above, the Council's risk management strategy reflects the view that risk management is an integral part of corporate governance.

In July 2002 the Council formally adopted a framework for corporate govern-ance that was based upon the CIPFA (2001) guidelines, and the risk management strategy has evolved over time but continues to reflect these underlying principles. The objectives of the Council's risk management strategy are defined as follows:

- Integrate risk management into the culture of the council.
- Manage risk in accordance with the practice.
- Anticipate and respond to changing social, political, environmental, legisla-tive and technological requirements.
- Prevent injury damage and losses and reduce the cost of risk.
- Raise awareness of the need for risk management by all those connected with the council's delivery of services.

(Birmingham City Council, 2007)

Council documentation defines risk in terms of an event/series of events which may, partially or fully, prevent the council from achieving its planned objectives. More positively, risk can expressed as a failure to take advantage of opportunities to optimize the achievement of planned objectives. Less formally, the Head of Birmingham Audit takes the view that 'risk management is very much looking at achieving your objectives and what's going to stop you … that's the way we sell it. It's part of helping them (Service Directors) to meet their targets and service plans and make it easier for them to see what's going to trip them up.'

The logical corollary to this definition of risk is that risk management is concerned with making the most of opportunities to achieve objectives. This is achieved through a combination of risk transfer, risk control and risk acceptance.

Roles and responsibilities for risk: senior management

Responsibility for the development and implementation of risk management systems across the organization lies with the 'Resources'[4] section of the council which is headed up by the Corporate Director of Resources (see Figure 7.1). This director is named as the 'officer champion' for corporate governance within the council, and the deputy leader is the equivalent 'members' champion. Senior management responsibility for risk management is built into the council's regulations, as Section 8 (Birmingham City Council, 2005) requires the directors to issue annual assurance statements on risk management and internal control. These statements form the basis for an annual statement on internal control which is signed off by the Chief Executive, the Leader of the Council, the Corporate Director of Resources and the Chief Legal Officer. It is interesting that this regulation, common to all councils applying the CIPFA governance guidelines, is more onerous than the private sector equivalent under the Cadbury Code. Members of the Board of Directors of companies are merely required to undertake an annual review of internal controls (including risk management) but they are *not* required to issue an assurance statement.

Roles and responsibilities for risk: internal audit

Day-to-day responsibility for the development and maintenance of the risk management processes rests with Birmingham Audit, which is the internal audit section of the council. Birmingham Audit emphasizes, however, that 'good governance requires that risk management is embedded into the culture of the organization, with members and managers at all levels recognizing that risk management is part of their job' (CIPFA, 2007). Risk management is therefore very definitely not the exclusive responsibility of internal audit staff. The nature of the responsibility of others within Birmingham City Council in relation to risk management will be discussed in depth in the next section of this case.

Historically, the work of the internal audit function within local authorities has been focused on the provision of assurance on the core financial framework and systems and the detection, investigation and prevention of fraud and corruption. Risk management, however, encompasses much more than financial controls and this raises questions about the most appropriate location for risk management within councils. As indicated, Birmingham has chosen to place responsibility within internal audit, but other councils take the view that risk management is essentially a performance management concern, and so the function lies there rather than with internal audit. Size is also a determining factor here, as some councils will not be of sufficient size to warrant a separate internal audit or risk management function.

In specifying the function that should hold supervisory responsibility for risk management it is important to avoid any conflict of interest in the work of the function. If internal audit staff are testing control effectiveness, then they should not simultaneously be involved in drafting those controls, or advising on them. In practical terms this means that separate teams of staff are required with different, clearly defined, areas of responsibility.

In Birmingham City Council the separation of duties is achieved by the internal audit section being split into those who conduct the internal audits per se, and a separate risk team who provide the broader support for the risk management system and its application across the different services in the council. Only 16 per cent of the work of internal audit is now allocated to the audit of financial systems, and the remainder is devoted to risk management, corporate governance and business/operational activities, although the latter does include an element of financial control review. The annual internal audit plans are prepared in accordance with the CIPFA Code of Practice for Internal Audit.

The creation of a specialist risk group is an explicit recognition of the size, complexity and diversity of risks encountered within the City Council, and the non-accounting nature of the work of this team is illustrated by the fact that they are training for the Institute of Internal Audit or Institute of Risk Management examinations rather than the management accounting focused CIMA examinations. This also reflects anecdotal evidence of the emergence of a new risk management 'profession'.

The risk team in internal audit are responsible for revising and updating the core risk management documents within the council: the Policy Statement, Risk Management Strategy, Risk Management Methodology and the Risk Management Toolkit, all of which are subject to both internal and external review. In addition, the team provides guidance and information to operational staff and strategic directors, as well as organizing risk training sessions and workshops. Working alongside staff from across the council's directorates, Birmingham Audit assist in the development of practical approaches to risk identification and monitoring via regular training sessions (Box 7.2).

Roles and responsibilities for risk: council staff and members

Figure 7.1 depicts the management team. Figure 7.2 shows the overall structure of staff and members within Birmingham City Council. The members take the strategic decisions which reflect the council's long- and short-term objectives. As officers of the council, the senior management are then responsible for the overall implementation of these decisions, but the day-to-day operational management falls within the individual directorates. Directorates are further broken down into divisions which subdivide into specific services or business units. In principle, it is therefore possible to plot the risk of any given action/decision, right down from the members to the individuals who are working in that area. The aim is to ensure that all parties throughout the hierarchy communicate about risks – the existence, scale, likelihood, consequences, tools for control, etc. – and that the risk management framework ensures that risks are regularly monitored and reviewed. Both the communication and monitoring processes are two way: from members down to service staff and vice versa. Risk management can only be truly described as embedded when risk awareness and understanding permeates all of the organization relatively equally, so that all staff recognize it as part of their job and are working towards optimizing the achievement of objectives.

Implementation of the principles that underpin the risk management strategy as described above requires the establishment of a very clear framework which incorporates all of the processes that are involved in managing risks.

Box 7.2 Training in risk identification and control

Training in how to identify and monitor risks can start at a very basic level. For example, at a training session for new staff in Birmingham, members of the risk team within internal audit gave the trainees the task of getting a raw egg – unsupported – from one side of a large room to the other, without breaking it. To help them in the process, teams were provided with access to any materials that they might wish to use from the department's stationery cupboard. Most of the teams were very concerned about the risk associated with the fragility of the egg, and so spent a lot of time building structures from cardboard, paper, string and various other items to minimize the risk of breakage. The exercise ended with two members of the risk team throwing an unprotected egg from end to end of the room, and simply being careful in the process of catching it. The lesson learnt was that it is easy to overestimate risk, and also to spend a lot of money on protecting against it. The management of risk requires the ability to take a perspective on its importance, and hence how much to spend on managing it.

This particular training session took place within the offices of Birmingham audit; training is also organized on site within the services themselves. Head of Service and other line managers may request assistance from internal audit to help them identify and evaluate the risks that they may encounter based upon the service plan that they have drafted. The assistance does not take the form of telling them what risks may exist, but simply helps them to think about what might get in the way of the achievement of the plan's objectives. To some extent, risk management is about a particular mind set, and after staff have had some practice at going through the process of risk identification and assessment several times, many become adept at the process. At this point it can be argued that risk management is starting to become embedded within the culture and thinking of the organization.

The risk management framework

Standard models of risk management commonly break down the process into five core stages. This basic sequence is illustrated in Figure 7.3, which is based upon the risk standard developed by the Institute of Risk Management (2002).

Within Birmingham City Council, the risk management methodology is broken down into five component parts as follows:

- Risk/opportunity and identification.
- Risk/opportunity and analysis.
- Risk/opportunity prioritization.
- Management of risks/opportunities.
- Monitoring progress.

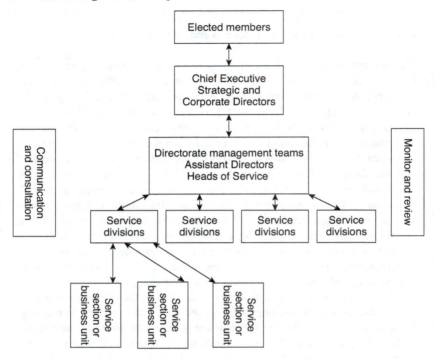

Figure 7.2 Council-wide responsibilities for risk

Source: Adapted from Birmingham City Council (2007), appendix 2

Figure 7.3 Core elements of the risk management process

Source: Adapted from Institute of Risk Management (2002)

The language used by Birmingham City Council varies little from that within the standard model of the Institute of Risk Management. In this section we will look briefly at each of these stages.

Risk/opportunity identification

Risks and opportunities are defined in terms of the aim of achieving the council's objectives in relation to service provision. Many different types of risk may be identified and the causes are likely to be various and sometimes specific to individual services. Internal audit suggest a prompt list of risks that staff may wish to consider, including environmental, legal, political, financial, social, reputational, managerial, physical, and technological risks.

Every service area is required to identify risks and opportunities against the background of its service objectives, and all risks are then recorded on a risk register, which acts as a key reference point for the entire risk management system. An example of a risk register is shown in Table 7.3 to illustrate how the whole framework ties together. Box 7.3 illustrates the breadth of risks that may be faced within an individual service area, and formally recorded on the risk register. *Note:* the risks in this example are for illustrative purposes only.

It is also important to note that the need for risk identification and management is not exclusive to the service level of the council. Directorates and the broader corporate level of the council will also face risks which may be either independent of, or interact with, the service level risks. A good example of this is in relation to the performance measures within the CPA (or CAA) assessment. Birmingham City Council acknowledge that CPA was one of the factors motivating the adoption of risk management, and the CPA rating is important to both resourcing and reputation, and so close attention is paid to ensuring that the necessary performance targets are achieved.

For example, if the council's plan includes the aim to move up the CPA rating scale, it will compile a list of the areas where performance requires improvement in order for the specified targets be achieved. It may be that certain performance

---

Box 7.3 Example: library service

Risks may include:

- Failure to comply with legislation on disability access.
- Theft of books/DVDs/CDs.
- Under performing on level of library use for the CPA target.
- Poor security of buildings which may increase the risk of burglary.
- Lack of funding to offer Internet facilities at neighbourhood libraries, despite a promise to do so in the current 3-year plan.

targets are critical to the CPA score. For example, within the audit commission's weighting system, social services are particularly important, and so high performance in this area is critical. From a corporate perspective this may imply that performance targets within social services become a high level risk because they can make the difference between achieving or not achieving the CPA objectives. In practical terms, this means that the performance moves up from being a service or directorate level risk, to become a corporate risk, because it affects the overall position of the council. Under such circumstances, the risk may well be classed as severe and become the focus of significant management attention and monitoring.

Knowing the possible risks that may be faced is, however, insufficient for control purposes. More information is required to know where to prioritize the control effort and where risks are too small to really matter.

Risk/opportunity analysis

After risks have been identified, they are grouped and ranked according to the likelihood of their occurrence and their expected impact. Likelihood/impact matrices are commonly used by risk managers. The exact design of the matrices will vary from organization to organization but the underlying principle remains identical: the aim is to be able to classify risks in terms of the two dimensions. In Birmingham they have four classes of likelihood and four of impact. These are high, significant, medium and low. Tables 7.1 and 7.2 detail the definitions applicable to each of these classifications. At this stage in the process, the risks being classified are the inherent risks, i.e. those which may occur assuming no management controls are in place to reduce their likelihood or impact.

Risk/opportunity prioritization

Figure 7.4 shows the classification process that is used to prioritize risks or opportunities. Risks are marked on to the 4 × 4 matrix according to the classification of low to high likelihood and low to high impact. The shaded zones of the matrix equate to a traffic light system: severe is a red light, material is amber, and tolerable is green. The definitions of these zones directly reflect the severity of impact upon service objectives if the risk crystallizes, and the degree of severity is

Table 7.1 Likelihood

Classification	Definition
High	Almost certain in most circumstances. Higher than 80% probability.
Significant	Likely. 50% to 80% probability.
Medium	Possible. 20%–50% probability.
Low	Unlikely but could occur at any time. Less than 20% probability.

Table 7.2 Impact

Classification	Definition
High	Critical to achievement of objectives. Huge impact on cost/reputation and requiring a long-term recovery plan.
Significant	Major impact on costs and objectives. Serious impact on reputation or quality extending into the medium/long-term.
Medium	Waste of time and resources but with moderate impact and potentially expensive medium-term effects.
Low	Minor loss/costs/inconvenience. Short- or medium-term impact only.

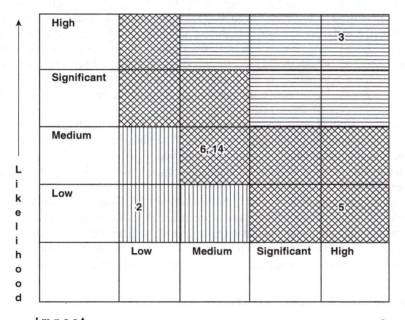

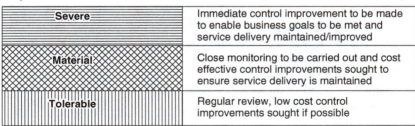

Figure 7.4 Risk/opportunity prioritization matrix

Source: Birmingham City Council, Risk Management Methodology, November 2007

reflected in the subsequent level of control and frequency of monitoring. For example, in Figure 7.4 risk No. 2 is classed as being of lower severity and low likelihood. As a result, the level of control over this risk is likely to be low, because the impact is also likely to be low. In contrast, risk No. 3 is classed as being both high risk and high likelihood and hence severe. In terms of the definitions, this means that there is a strong likelihood of the risk occurring and jeopardizing the achievement of council objectives. The only way to resolve this is to immediately introduce additional control systems.

All risks with a high impact and significant or above likelihood are classified as severe, and information about these risks and the related controls are automatically escalated up to the next level in the organizational hierarchy. In other words, if a service manager sees something as a severe risk, this fact will be made known to the service director, who then has a responsibility to ensure that controls and action plans are devised to reduce that residual risk to material rather than severe. Severe risks, which represent five of the sixteen elements of the matrix, are the subject of both weekly meetings and action plans within the relevant directorate. The action plans provide a record of the effectiveness of existing controls, who is responsible for managing the specific risk and the nature and timing of the subsequent control actions taken (see below).

Risks identified as having medium impact or below and with only a low likelihood of occurrence are classed as tolerable. Tolerable risks are regularly reviewed and low cost risk reduction strategies identified where possible, but they are not proactively managed as they are seen as acceptable within the existing management routines.

An additional matrix of risks is drafted in terms of residual exposure levels. All residual risks are 'owned' by a named member of staff and the residual risks are regularly reported and compared to the target risk, which is defined as the long term desired level of risk in the specific service area. The risk matrix for each service thus acts as both a feedback and feed-forward control for monitoring purposes.

Management and control of risks

There are six stages involved in the process of the management of risk. These are as follows:

- Establishing the risk appetite.
- Selecting whether to accept, control, modify, transfer or eliminate the risk.
- Recording the reasons for the decision.
- Implementing the decision.
- Assigning individual ownership to each risk.
- Completion of an action plan.

Risks are expressed and measured in terms of their impact upon the council's objectives and they are managed in terms of the council's risk appetite. The risk appetite reflects the extent of risk which is deemed to be acceptable or tolerable.

Tolerable is defined in terms of the traffic light system used in the matrix on page 141. Once identified and prioritized, risks are therefore managed through acceptance, control, modification or transfer. The aim is to bring the residual risk level down to a level classed as tolerable.

In choosing how to respond to a particular risk, staff must take into account the trade-off between the cost of controls and the costs incurred if objectives are not achieved. In crude terms, spending £100,000 on anti-burglary protection makes little economic sense if the maximum loss from the burglary is estimated at £70,000. The cost of implementing and operating a control should not normally exceed the maximum potential benefit.

Once a decision has been made on how a risk will be controlled, individuals are assigned ownership of the risk and take responsibility for monitoring progress against controls, to ensure that the risk remains within tolerable levels and does not threaten the achievement of objectives. Feedback from the monitoring is then used to review and possibly modify both the objectives and modify the control process itself.

Internal audit complements the monitoring by checking whether the risk controls are working effectively, thus fulfilling the role as shown on the right hand side of Figure 7.3. Birmingham Audit is using a risk-based approach which prioritizes those directorates and service areas which may carry significant 'corporate' level risks as well as operational risks.

Monitoring progress

The risk registers, allocation of risk ownership and action plans all form important parts of the risk management process, but ultimately risks are only managed if the process is continuous, and this requires that the risks and action plans are the subject of regular review.

Risk registers are reviewed at least quarterly to ensure that risks are deleted, added or upgraded as appropriate. Where a risk is deleted, there is a requirement that the reasons for the deletion are fully recorded, together with an explanation of what has happened to the risk. The mechanisms adopted to review risks may be selected by service or directorate managers, and may take the form of an agenda item at a management meeting, a special risk meeting, or a workshop organized through internal audit.

Complementing the risk registers are the action plans, which also require regular updating and monitoring. There is a need to make sure that the chosen actions are proving effective in managing risks or taking advantage of opportunities, or there is a danger that service objectives will not be achieved.

Ensuring consistency in applying the risk management framework

Consistency in the application of the risk management framework is achieved via the use of common training programmes and standardized documentation for the recording and management of all risks throughout the council. Consistency is also monitored by the internal audit process itself, with staff knowledgeable about which directorates or service areas are more/less focused on risk management issues, and good/bad at maintaining up to date risk information. Two of the most important documents are the risk register and the action plan, which are illustrated and discussed below.

The risk register in Table 7.3 contains two illustrative risks for a specific service. The main points to note in the design of the document are that the elements of risk identification, prioritization and management are implicitly linked. At the same time, the distinction between intrinsic and residual risk levels makes clear the impact of the control system. A common document across all services also ensures that when risks are aggregated across the whole council, internal audit can be certain that equivalent approaches have been adopted in all directorates.

The action plan (Table 7.4) forces staff to face up to the need to monitor risks in order to keep them under control. In other words, the aim is to see risk identification and measurement as a perpetual cycle rather than an irregular event. By being forced to record the decisions taken, the basis for them, and ensure that controls are regularly reviewed for effectiveness, people become answerable for their actions and begin to understand the link between risk and performance.

Information support systems for risk management

Information and Communications Technology is fundamentally important to the maintenance of the risk management control system in Birmingham because the

Table 7.3 Risk register: example

Directorate/Division/Project:
Date:

Risk/opportunity information			Counter-measures		
No.	Description of risk/opportunity and risk/ opportunity owner	Inherent risk (likelihood/ impact)	Description of current controls/ mitigation in place and date when controls last reviewed and reported upon	Residual risk (likelihood/ impact)	Further controls proposed and date for implementation
2	Failure to comply with new legislation Mr R. Xxxx	Significant/ high	Staff advice and training	Low/ significant	Staff briefings to keep people informed of new legislation
6	Failure to improve service	High/medium	Awaiting corporate direction	Review services Medium/medium	

Source: Birmingham City Council, Risk Management Methodology, 2007

Table 7.4 Action plan

Objective influenced by the risk/opportunity	Inherent risk likelihood/impact		
Risk/opportunity description	Residual risk likelihood/impact		
	Residual risk accepted?	Yes	No
Consequences (e.g. effects on service provision, people, money, reputation)	If residual risk not accepted what approach has been agreed?	Transfer risk	Eliminate risk
		Control risk	Modify risk
Risk/opportunity owner and reference number	Target risk likelihood/impact		
Description of current actions being taken to mitigate the risk, including the responsible officer and date when the controls were last reviewed to assess their effectiveness	Further agreed control measures to be applied, including responsible officer and deadline for completion		

Source: Birmingham City Council, Risk Management Methodology, 2007

technology is integral to the risk control process. In the early stages of the development of the risk management systems, documentation and risk guidance was posted on the intranet, but it was felt that its usefulness for risk management purposes was limited. As a result, the risk team chose to purchase Magique, a dedicated piece of commercial risk management software. The team was also responsible for the system's installation. The role of Magique is fourfold:

- *Training.* Online training packages help to get the risk message across to staff at all levels within the council, whilst simultaneously easing the pressure on staff resources within internal audit.
- *Real-time update of risk registers.* Magique is not fully operational across the full council yet, and so real time updates remain an objective rather than a fully realized system, although the importance of making progress in this regard is well recognized. Real time updating ensures that up to date council wide risk registers are continuously available to both internal audit and senior council staff. The software does not, however, automatically update the internal audit plan in response to changes in the service level risk registers. Instead these have to be completed manually by internal audit staff.
- *Maintenance of an events log.* The events log is used for both audit planning and the redesign of risk controls to reduce the likelihood of future events.

- *Management of cross-directorate risk information.* By granting real-time access to information across all services, the software facilitates the management of cross-directorate risk information. For example, the council's CPA score is aggregated from across a broad range of council activities and senior management therefore need to be aware of the risk of the score changing because of shifts in risk data across all of the relevant directorates. Magique enables analysis of cross directorate information, because it can present slices of risk profiles both vertically and horizontally across the organization.

Magique therefore enables internal audit to pull together all of the information needed to draft the annual assurance statement on risk management and internal control. In the absence of such technology, the database would have to be maintained manually, and the preparation of the assurance statement would clearly be more time consuming.

The interdependencies between service delivery, ICT and risk management can be usefully illustrated by reference to the scope for using a data warehouse for data matching and anti-fraud work. This is separate from Magique but is an example of using ICT to manage fraud risk, for example, within the benefits section of Birmingham City Council. One of the benefits that is available to people living in the city is a reduction in the amount of Council Tax payable for one person households. Sharing information across directorates and other public agencies can help to reduce the high risk of fraudulent claims for this benefit. ICT can facilitate this information sharing by enabling cross-referencing of the information provided by individuals to different sections of the council e.g. housing benefit and the electoral register. One benefit of the investment in ICT is thus that it frees up the time of fraud control staff.

The big challenge: linking risk to performance management

In its training sessions for staff, Birmingham Audit define risk as follows:

> The threat that an event or action will adversely affect an organization's ability to achieve its objectives.

and they note that:

> One of life's certainties and how successful organizations can deal with it can have a major impact on the achievement of their key business goals.
>
> (Audit Commission, 2001)

Risk and organizational objectives are intrinsically linked, and the challenge in practice is to make the link work and demonstrate this by *proven* improvements in performance.

For Birmingham City Council, the challenge of demonstrating how risk management works to help achieve objectives is potentially made even more difficult by the fact that it is a public sector body and also a political organization. As a public sector organization serving a huge and diverse community, the council's risks extend beyond the financial and reputational ones to include issues of public safety, community health and also political risks. In addition, council objectives are determined by elected members, although the day-to-day management is largely done by paid officers. In the words of the Chief Executive:

> for the Council, we're not just talking about ourselves but we're sort of seen as part of the City as a whole, so it's about reputational risk for the City. And then of course there are issues which are simply to do with the politics of the place. It is a political organization essentially, and therefore members are particularly exercised about how their actions are seen, in a way that the private sector wouldn't worry so much about.

All of this means that the council's corporate plan is very wide ranging in scope. The 2007–10 Performance Plan states that:

> Our vision is to create a global city with a local heart, a cleaner, greener and safer city that is a magnet for business investment and job creation. The City Council aims to be one of the best run local authorities in England, recognized for its excellent services and the efficient use of its money, people and assets, enabling all our richly diverse communities to benefit from a better quality of life.

The vision is admirable, but needs to be 'translated' into specific objectives which can be applied to all of the directorates and services across the council, and pulled together by the identification of the corporate support objectives. This is done by applying the performance planning framework portrayed in Figure 7.5, which shows how the different levels of plan – city, council, directorate, local constituencies and the broader local area are tied together to form a coherent whole. The overall coherence, and the council's potential/capacity to achieve these aims are the subject of the Audit Commission's corporate area assessment.

The last row of the table is particularly important because it highlights the responsibility of all members of staff to understand the council's objectives and the role that they play individually in helping to achieve them. Risk management forms part of that role.

The details of how responsibilities for performance are distributed across the council is contained in Figure 7.6.

The performance plan for 2007–10 is a 40-page, publicly available document that details the objectives in terms of both strategic themes – such as 'safe city' – and also directorates. Performance against the plan is highly visible, because the council publishes an annual plan that indicates which targets were achieved and

Our planning framework

Taking Birmingham Forward
Developed with the Birmingham Strategic Partnership, this describes the vision for the future of our city and action plans to achieve improvements.

The Council Plan	Constituency Community Plans	Major Plans	Local Area Agreement
Translates Taking Birmingham Forward into action for the Council, sets priorities and targets for services.	Priorities, service targets, improvement and consultation plans for each constituency.	A set of plans developed by the key agencies working together to shape and improve services across the city.	A set of targets agreed with local partners and with central government, allowing us greater local flexibility and freedom to innovate to achieve the city's vision. These are its themes: • Safer and Stronger Communities • Children and Young People • Healthier Communities and Older People • Enterprise and Economic Development

Financial Plans
Set out the financial resources available to deliver services and support priorities.

Performance Plan
Sets clear targets for each priority in the Council Plan and allocates responsibilities for measures to monitor progress and hold us to account.

Directorate Plans
Translate council priorities and targets into detailed actions and objectives for each service.

Work Plans and Performance & Development Reviews (PDRs)
Detailed plans for all teams and employees ensure that everyone knows what is expected of them and how their work contributes to meeting council priorities.

Figure 7.5 Planning framework

Source: Performance Plan, 2007–10

People/group	We gather data	We check data independently	We explain and justify performance	We secure data quality and robustness	We are accountable for performance	We propose measure and improvement actions	We lead and implement agreed improvement activity	We track improvements	We challenge measures, results and improvement actions	We jointly solve problems and share learning	We approve information and follow-up actions	We make in-depth reviews of performance	We review performance management systems and propose improvements	We make in-depth reviews of under-performing areas	We implement outcomes of service reviews	We monitor progress in implementing outcomes of service reviews	We maintain the corporate performance system	We manage the corporate performance system
Directorates	✓	✓	✓	✓	✓	✓	✓	✓	✓	✓		✓	✓	✓	✓	✓	✓	
Corporate Policy and Performance Team		✓		✓					✓	✓			✓	✓	✓		✓	✓
Strategic Directors				✓	✓	✓	✓											
Corporate Management Team								✓	✓	✓	✓					✓		
Strategic Directors peer reviews										✓	✓							
Deputy Leader					✓			✓	✓	✓								
Executive Management Team					✓	✓		✓	✓	✓		✓				✓		
Cabinet				✓		✓		✓		✓	✓							
Excellence Board						✓						✓	✓	✓				
Business Transformation						✓			✓				✓	✓				
Overview and Scrutiny Committees						✓			✓			✓		✓		✓		
Internal Audit		✓		✓		✓												
Performance Management Network													✓					
Planning Team				✓			✓	✓	✓	✓	✓	✓	✓		✓			
Strategic Finance Officers Group	✓		✓	✓				✓	✓	✓	✓							✓
Budget & Efficiency Group		✓					✓	✓	✓			✓	✓			✓		
Cabinet Office		✓						✓	✓					✓		✓		
Delivery Support Unit						✓										✓		

Figure 7.6 Responsibilities within the performance framework

Source: Performance Plan, 2007–10

Birmingham City Council
Our performance against the targets set out in the 2007/08 Performance Plan
Children, Young Peoples and Families Portfolio

Priority	Dir.	PI Ref No.	Measure description	Performance Aim	Return Format	Actual	Target	Status	Comments
1.3.	CYP&F	CYP56a	Percentage of 16 year olds achieving 5 or more A*-C GCSEs or equivalent, including English and maths	Bigger is Better	%	41.8	45	◢	Although the target was not achieved, results improved by a further 1% this year on top of the 2% improvement last year. The rate of improvement is above the national average. There is a new national floor target for all schools to achieve at least 30% 5A*-C including English and maths by 2011/12. All schools have now set targets of at least 30% and those schools that are currently below the target will have individual action plans agreed with the LA by this summer.
1.3.	CYP&F	CH20/LPSA11	Percentage of 16–18 year olds *not* in education, employment or training	Smaller is Better	%	7.34	7.5	☆	The final result for this LPSA measure is taken at November 2007. At that point in time the proportion of young people aged 16–18 not in employment, education or training (NEET) had been reduced from 10.31% to 7.34% against an LPSA target of 7.5% in Birmingham. For the twelve months, November 2006 to November 2007, this amounts to a reduction in numbers of young people recorded as NEET from 3436 down to 2583 (LPSA target 7.0%). At a time when key pressures (eastern European migration, age discrimination legislation etc) are effectively squeezing the availability of opportunities for young people, this is a remarkable achievement that is unlikely to be rivalled in similar urban settings.
2.4.	CYP&F	CH19/CYP08	Number of children and young people are first time entrants to Criminal Justice Service	Smaller is Better	Number	2106	2352	☆	The Service's data has identified a year on year increase of reprimands mostly due to the Sanction detection targets which may reduce following the recent Flannagan Report. The IYSS will build on the targeted nature of our preventative strategies. Service continues to have strong partnership arrangements with the YISP and YIP and is hopeful to recruit to the 5 ASB posts that have been funded by the Youth taskforce and YJB and have evidenced positive outcomes for young people subject to ABC's and ASBO's

(a)

Birmingham City Council
Our performance against the targets set out in the 2007/08 Performance Plan

Portfolio:	Status Measure ☆		Status Measure ●		Status Measure ◢		Not yet available
Children, Young People and Families	Indicators	Milestones	Indicators	Milestones	Indicators	Milestones	
Performance Plan Measures 2007–08	3	0	0	0	3	0	0
Totals by status measure	☆ 3		● 0		◢ 3		0

(b)

Key: ☆ Target exceeded   ● On track   ◢ Target at risk

Figure 7.7 Performance report (a) Performance report (b)

which were not. An example of this performance reporting is included in Figure 7.7, which illustrates that in the 2006–7 financial year the children, young people and families directorate exceeded on three of its objectives, was on track for a further six, but another six were at risk. This performance information provides feedback for the risk management process. The objectives identified as being at risk will be prioritized in terms of their management, particularly if they are classed as severe within the risk management system. As already noted, severe means that the implications for achievement of objectives are significant and the consequences high.

The link between planning, delivery and monitoring of performance is illustrated below in Figure 7.8. This is not taken from the council's own documentation, but is a generic example of how a council's plans and scorecards for performance can be cascaded downwards from the very general vision, as quoted earlier, into individual performance plans for every member of staff. If the performance plans also include risk plans which specify where the responsibility for risk lies, then risk becomes part of the mechanism by which performance is evaluated. The risk and performance functions then run in tandem, and it can truly be said that risk management is embedded into the organization. This is the ultimate aim.

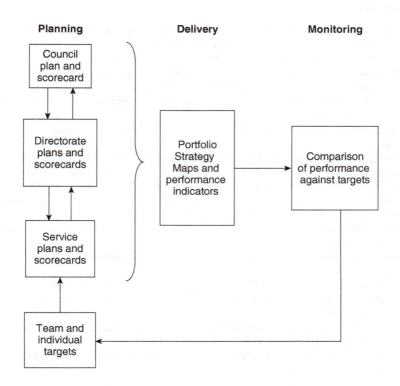

Figure 7.8 The performance management control loop

Conclusion

Birmingham City Council is a huge and complex organization with wide ranging social, economic and political objectives. Establishing the objectives and then establishing the necessary control systems to achieve them is a massive operation. Risk management is a fundamental element of the broader management control system and is particularly strongly linked to performance management because risk is defined in terms of the ability to achieve objectives.

The risk team within internal audit have created a very formal, well documented and structured framework for risk management, and its effectiveness as a control tool is reported upon annually. In the end, that effectiveness is driven not by the system itself but by the people who implement it – the council members and staff. Risk management is only as good as the people who implement it, but the local government sector in the UK has gone through something of a performance management revolution since 1999 and the introduction of Best Value. That revolution has been accompanied by a step change in the quality of risk management, and, as investment in systems continues to increase, the hope is that even more progress will be made.

References

Airmic, IRM and ALARM (2002) *A Risk Management Standard*, London.

Audit Commission (2001) *Worth the Risk: Improving Risk Management in Local Government*, Audit Commission, London.

Audit Commission (2006) *Briefing on the Audit Commission's Comprehensive Performance Assessment Frameworks*, Audit Commission, London.

Audit Commission (2007) *Corporate Assessment, Birmingham City Council*, Audit Commission, London, February.

Birmingham City Council (2007a) *Delivering Good Governance in Local Government*, London.

Birmingham City Council (2007b) Risk Management Strategy, revised November 2007.

Birmingham City Council (2009a) Volume B, Essential Documents supporting the Constitution, Volume B, Part 4(C), Management Structure (revised May 2009).

Birmingham City Council (2009b) Briefing Note, http://www.cipfa.org.uk/panels/corporate_governance/good_gov_briefing.cfm

CIPFA (2001) *Corporate Governance in Local Government: A Keystone for Community Governance Framework*, London.

Committee of Sponsoring Organizations of the Treadway Commission (COSO) (2004) *Enterprise Risk Management – Integrated Framework*, AICPA, New York.

Crawford, M. and Stein, W. (2004) 'Risk management in UK local authorities: the effect of current guidance and practice', *International Journal of Public Sector Management*, Vol. 17, pp. 498–512.

OPM/CIPFA (2004) *Good Governance Standard for Public Services*, Office for Public Management and CIPFA, London.

Standards Australia (2004) *Australian and New Zealand Risk Management Standard AS/NZS 4360:2004*, 3rd edn.

Part IV
Key lessons for the future

8 Lessons from the case studies

Aim

The aim of this chapter is to review the different styles of risk management presented in the four case studies, and use them to identify the core drivers of effective enterprise risk management. This involves asking the difficult question 'How does an organization embed risk management into its culture?' The question extends beyond the issue of which standard or regulation to follow and into the realms of how to apply a set of broad principles within a specific context. The answer will therefore be different for each organization, but this chapter highlights the factors that managers need to be conscious of in building their risk management system. The chapter is structured as follows:

- Overview of the case studies.
- Risk management in context.
- The big challenge: implementing a three-dimensional system.
- Lessons from the public sector.

Overview of the case studies

Awareness of risk management as a discipline is at an all time high. At the same time, because both private and public sector organizations have to meet the needs of an increasingly diverse range of stakeholders, risk is no longer solely a financial concern. The case studies show that it is increasingly the norm for organizations to look more broadly at non-financial risks and seek to embed their management at an operational level. This broadening out of risk management directly reflects the shift in thinking in the discipline since the world's first risk standard was published in 1995. Enterprise risk management seems to now be the generally accepted approach, although how it is effected in practice remains under researched.

In demonstrating that high profile organizations take to heart the need to establish a process for understanding and managing risks, the cases also highlight some consistency of approach across organizations, combined with differences in detail. By focusing on the differences, it may be possible to learn some useful lessons about how to create a more effective risk management system.

All four organizations, both public and private sector, use specific processes to monitor risks, and feedback systems which facilitate appropriate ways of handling them. In each case, some form of internal audit team provides either an oversight function or acts as an expert link in that feedback loop. These more formal risk monitoring teams and the controls they devise to manage risks are important, but the case studies also highlight the need to embed risk management within more easily understood behaviours, consistent with the overall organizational culture. Frontline staff, managers and specialists should be completely aligned on risk, in part just to ensure that there is a consistency of approach. They should understand instinctively that good performance includes good risk management. It is in these softer, less formalized aspects of risk management that the approaches used by the organizations are very different.

Tesco, with a relatively straightforward business model and easily identifiable risks, aims to keep bureaucracy to a minimum. Royal Bank of Scotland (RBS) faces far more complex risks, is much more heavily regulated – and has a distinct 'risk community' of specialists numbering more than 4,000 strong. Birmingham City Council has incorporated risk management into its core service delivery approach, and the Department for Culture, Media and Sport (DCMS) uses a highly structured risk framework to manage projects that cross divisions and feature a host of third parties. In effect, the four organizations can be regarded as points along a spectrum of risk management approaches that ranges from almost entirely compliance focused at one end, to minimally bureaucratic and performance focused at the other.

Risk management in context

In Chapters 2 and 3 we saw that a risk management system is not designed in a vacuum – it needs to be appropriate to both the external context within which the organization operates, such as the governance regulations, and the internal context in terms of the nature of the business, organizational structure, etc. Risk management is all about assisting in the achievement of organizational objectives and supporting the development and implementation of strategy. Its processes are aimed at translating high level strategies into lower level attainable operational objectives by allocating responsibility for risks across the entire organization. This means that organizational culture – the style of control, the way in which performance is measured and rewarded, the overall ethos – will be reflected in the risk management system. Engendering a sense of risk awareness is potentially a massive cultural challenge.

As illustrated in Table 8.1, the case study organizations clearly operate in very different contexts, which therefore impact upon the design of their risk management systems. The table goes some way towards explaining the differences in approach resulting from the variations in certain aspects of context that can be identified in the case studies.

Tesco is an extremely successful business, thanks in part to a coherent strategy that drives every part of the organization. The company's core objective is very

Table 8.1 Case study context

Tesco	RBS	Birmingham City Council	DCMS
Complexity of business			
Relatively low: buy and distribute goods; marketing; managing cash	High: multiple business lines, all with varying levels of risk	High: multiple stakeholders combined with interdependent risks	High: multiple stakeholders combined with interdependent risks
Key risks			
Robustness of processes	Financial, compliance	Political and social, compliance, reputation	Political and social, compliance, reputation
Level of external regulation			
Moderate	High	Moderate to high	Moderate

clearly defined in terms of customer satisfaction. Tesco's staff, from CEO to shelf-filler, are focused on building customer loyalty. External factors such as competitor activity might affect decision making at the periphery, but the board feels that shareholder value flows from operational efficiencies designed to help its own people exceed customer expectations.

As a simple business – buying and distributing goods, marketing and managing cash – Tesco's principal risks centre on the robustness of its processes. Any failure in the supply chain, for example, damages the business in the eyes of customers, so any risks to its smooth operation must be identified and managed. A relatively flat structure helps. Although it employs almost 470,000 people, Tesco only has five levels of management, so accountability for risks is generally very clear.

Tesco has a standard governance hierarchy (Figure 4.1) – a top-level board of directors controlling strategy, supported by more operationally focused subsidiary boards and functional committees. There is no distinction between the UK and overseas businesses, which ensures strong consistency of processes for strategy and risk management. At the centre of these committees and teams sits the Tesco 'steering wheel' (Figure 4.2), its own version of the balanced scorecard; this plays a vital role in linking key strategic objectives into KPIs that connect to day-to-day operations. The steering wheel works to manage risks from two directions. It ensures staff and management are clear about their objectives – shop workers can see exactly what's expected of them, for example, in terms of in-store customer experience and understand how risks can devalue their performance. And it helps senior management quickly identify areas where objectives are not being met so they can be addressed. This ensures that risk management is invisible and directly linked to performance management but remains fundamental to the business.

In contrast, RBS runs a much more complex business and as a bank it faces some of the sternest challenges in risk management. Their core competency is protecting money, but as a listed company they are evaluated on their ability to profit from taking complex risks. Recent events have thrown these issues into a stark light, particularly for large banks like RBS which engage in both straight-forward banking and in exploiting risk to generate returns across multiple jurisdictions. It would seem that the biggest problem for risk management in banking is how to manage the seemingly conflicting objectives of compliance with capital adequacy rules whilst simultaneously generating profits that match market expectations.

RBS is subject to substantive external monitoring in relation to risk: Sarbanes Oxley, the Combined Code, the Basel capital adequacy rules and ARROW (the Advanced, Risk Responsive Operating FrameWork) to name but a few. The rapid growth of complex and exotic financial instruments has further complicated things. RBS has a well staffed risk management function which more than doubled in size in the two years leading up to the financial crisis. Where it differs from Tesco is in the bureaucratization and quantification of risk management, and the creation of silos managed by experts – such as credit risk, market risk, etc. The silos mirror the regulatory reporting framework, but seem to have only weak links into the day-to-day operations of the bank. It would seem that the risk management system in RBS was made captive and then 'strangled' by its external context.

Both of the public sector bodies, Birmingham City Council and the DCMS are shown in Table 8.1 as operating complex businesses that are subject to a moderate level of external monitoring. The two organizations are accountable to a wide range of stakeholders, including both funders and users of their services. They have developed structured approaches to risk management in response to new public management initiatives that began in central government but mirrored private sector guidelines. The risk improvement programme rolled out by central government in 2004 incorporated best practice from the private sector and bench-marks from a variety of public sector and commercial organizations around the world. The programme, filtered down to local government, emphasizes the need to specify objectives – primarily in terms of levels of service provision – and use risk management as a tool to manage threats and opportunities that may affect their achievement. As such, public sector risk management is performance oriented.

Political risks, in terms of changes in policies and/or government are hugely important at both local and central government level. Political accountability requires the delivery of annual assurance statements which form the basis of the mandated review of internal control. Consequently, clearly articulated risk management strategies and support structures are in place in both Birmingham City Council and the DCMS. At the same time, democratic accountability creates a sensitivity to the need to deliver agreed levels of service, enhanced by a recognition that the consequences of failure to deliver can be catastrophic e.g. in relation to child protection.

There are two key differences in context between the public and private sector cases. The first is that certain types of service provision are not a matter of choice for publicly funded organizations. They cannot simply decide not to offer a service if it creates problems for them, because of a need to comply with statutory requirements. In contrast, private sector companies can select fields of business which reflect their risk appetite, avoiding areas seen a too high a risk. Second, many public sector services are interdependent, creating portfolio level risks that are more difficult to manage. In many respects, therefore, public sector risk management is more complex than private sector risk management. Nonetheless, the case of Birmingham City Council illustrates that they have recognized and prioritized the creation of systems that tie risk and service delivery performance together at the operational level. As we shall see later, this offers some useful lessons for the private sector.

Looking across all four case studies, the internal context in terms of which organizational objectives are prioritized and how this affects risk management style is also important to consider. Tesco, Birmingham City Council and the DCMS all place the customer – or service user – as a priority. Tesco and Birmingham also create review and reward systems that link staff at all levels of the organization to the 'customer'. In this way, risk awareness becomes simultaneously linked to performance and also embedded. The DCMS, and especially RBS, have been less successful in this regard.

In summary, the context of each case study organization is very different and these differences feed through into the design of the risk management system. Contingency theory provides some useful insights into the idea that management control system design is not entirely a matter of free choice and some useful references include Chenhall (2003) and Woods (2009) but a detailed consideration of the theory is outside the scope of this book.

The big challenge: implementing a three-dimensional system

CIMA's publication *Risk Management: A Guide to Good Practice* (CIMA 2002) notes that risk management has traditionally been practised in a fragmented way, focusing on operational rather than strategic issues. Consequently, strategic risks have been managed reactively rather than proactively.

Shifting towards an enterprise-wide approach requires a willingness to move away from silo-based management in favour of a portfolio-based system of risk management. Directors and senior management need to recognize that interlinked operational activities create exposure to a portfolio of similarly interlinked risks. At all levels, managers therefore need to identify, measure and monitor the upside and downside risks that their decisions may create for the entire organization: the relationship between what goes on in one division or business unit and the organization's aggregate risk exposure must be clearly understood.

In the COSO 2004 framework, this type of integrated approach to risk management is depicted as a cube (see Figure 3.2) in which the three dimensions are:

- Organization objectives (strategic, operations, reporting and compliance).
- Organization structure (entity, subsidiaries, divisions, business units).
- Components on the internal control system (objectives, risk identification, assessment, response, control activities, communication and reporting and monitoring).

By implication, ERM requires successful integration across all three dimensions. In other words, all features of the internal control system for risk are in use at all levels of the organization in a way that reflects both the risk appetite and objectives. This is a big challenge – hence the title of this section.

The case studies show that the challenge of embedding risk management in this way is one which demands long-term commitment and a powerful corporate culture. If the board are setting objectives which middle or lower level managers do not understand, then ERM is not embedded as the relevant risks cannot be managed. Similarly, if staff are taking on risks that members of the Board of Directors do not understand, as in the case of certain banks, then ERM is not functioning effectively because risks are not being identified and controlled. Ultimately, what is needed is for high-level objectives to be clearly defined and converted into performance targets which are cascaded down through the organization, and supported via a risk management system that focuses on achievement of those targets.

There are strong parallels between performance management and risk management. They are both:

- Designed to ensure the achievement of corporate objectives.
- Organization wide in their scope.
- Designed to recognize organizational interdependences.
- The operational responsibility of line management.

The case studies of both Tesco and Birmingham City Council demonstrate that formalizing the links between performance and risk management can begin by using the strategic planning process to link strategy and performance across all levels of the organization.

Both cases provide illustrations of clear and simple statements of the organization's strategic focus, complemented by detail on how it will deliver its commitments under the plan and how it will measure success. In Tesco the steering wheel is the tool used for this process. In Birmingham City Council it works through the specification of service-level objectives and performance targets which are linked into the personal development plans for all staff. In this way, the corporate annual targets are tied into associated action plans which outline how all the various organizational activities contribute to the achievement of the strategies. Everyone is involved in developing performance plans.

In the case of Tesco, and any other organization that uses a performance management system such as the Balanced Scorecard, individual scorecards can be developed for each level of the organization. These cascade down from corporate level, through divisional and business units to the individual line managers. At each level the scorecards are underpinned by plans showing the link between strategic objectives and targeted outcomes. The scorecards may be complemented by strategy diagrams or maps which set out the plans and actions that will deliver the performance measured by the scorecards as well as the relevant performance targets.

Using scorecards which cascade down through the corporate hierarchy ensures ownership of targets and links them to the strategic plan. Recording the allocation of targets to individual managers in the performance database also provides an audit pathway for each performance indicator. The principle of cascading down responsibility for performance can also be applied to risk management.

Under ERM the underlying aim is to ensure that at all levels of an organization staff are:

- Aware of the risks that may affect performance in the areas over which they have responsibility.
- Take responsibility for management of those risks.
- Performance and risk monitoring work in parallel to ensure achievement of corporate objectives.

The strategic maps that define how performance targets will be achieved can be complemented by risk maps that identify the key threats to successful delivery at each level of the organization. In Birmingham, for example, the case shows that this was done by the creation of Directorate level risk maps. At the same time, responsibility for management of those risks can be specified by identifying 'owners' of risks, and including details of such ownership in the performance management system. In Birmingham, there are examples of both political (councillors) and staff ownership of risks. In other words, risk management and performance management can become fully integrated systems as illustrated in Figure 8.1.

Figure 8.1 shows that at all levels of the organization, from corporate down to the individual, objectives can be linked to both performance targets and risk maps. If a manager is hitting the performance targets, then he/she must simultaneously be managing the risks. If the performance targets are *not* linked across to risk maps, then there is a danger that performance will be achieved by taking on risks that exceed the organizational risk appetite.

Figure 8.1 shows how ERM integrates the three dimensions of objectives, structure and risk management controls. In Tesco this is reflected in the view expressed by the Head of International Audit that 'accountability for managing risk lies clearly with line managers'. The view is underpinned by a risk management system which is implicit rather than explicit. Not all of the case study organizations were so successful in this regard however. The evidence from

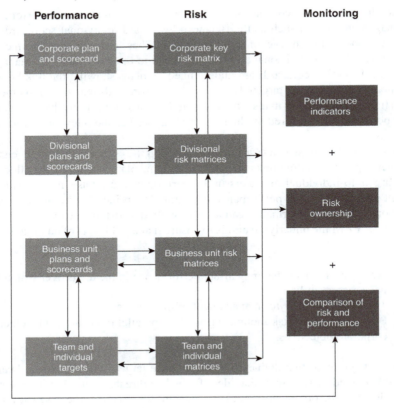

Figure 8.1 Integrating risk and performance management

DCMS shows that linking risk to performance across the entire department remains an ambition rather than a reality. In RBS, it is not clear whether there is a culture that is willing to pass responsibility for risk down the organization in this way. The function is highly centralized and assumes expertise, and performance is measured in terms of profit and rewarded accordingly, so that risk and performance may be severely out of line. This is a problem for all banks, and is the subject of ongoing debate amongst financial regulators (see for example, Treasury Committee, 2009). Additionally, the formal structures for risk management, based around silos which reflect the regulatory reporting systems for market, credit and operational risk respectively, indicate that compliance is the focus for the risk function in RBS, rather than performance. As a result, a massive and discrete risk management bureaucracy failed to identify, communicate and/or mitigate the effect of both localized and aggregate risks in the bank. Using a highly quantitatively based system for risk analysis, RBS ticked all the compliance boxes but that was not enough.

The extent to which risk is managed in silos rather than as part of an integrated whole is an interesting and challenging one. Some managers, for example, might take the view that in a global business such as Tesco, the risks from international operations are very different (and possibly higher) than from domestic operations. It may therefore be tempting to run discrete but parallel systems to manage domestic versus international risks. The case study shows that Tesco simply view the two arenas as complementary parts of the same business, and the risks therefore relate to Tesco as a whole and not just Tesco UK or Tesco Korea, etc. The risks are interdependent and so the business needs to be managed as a portfolio. Adopting this approach requires standardized procedures for risk management across the entire organization. This offers the benefit of highlighting situations where risks are higher, such as a specific geographic location, whilst simultaneously allowing direct comparison of risks across all units using a common framework.

A portfolio-based system of risk management also allows for the recognition of interdependent risks. For example, in Birmingham City Council, if the benefits section fails to process a claim sufficiently quickly, it may result in a family being made homeless for failure to pay their rent. This creates demand for a new service from a different section of the council, to provide temporary accommodation for that family. By recognizing that speed of processing in benefits reduces potential demand for services (and increased costs) for another department, a holistic system is developed. In the next section we show that the public sector can perhaps offer some lessons to the private sector on how to manage such interlinked risks.

Comparing the effectiveness of ERM implementation across the different cases, there is also some interesting evidence relating to the extent to which risk management is a value adding function. Tesco is widely perceived as a highly successful business and its market capitalization has increased from £32 billion in December 2006 to £34 billion in late 2010, an annualized growth rate of just over 2 per cent. A senior staff member is quoted in the case as stating that 'one of the reasons we are a successful business is because of risk management – people do it without knowing they are doing it. It is part of their accountabilities'. It is tricky to decide whether or not 2 per cent annual growth can be classed as successful, though when compared to performance in RBS, it is a massive achievement. RBS saw its market capitalization fall from £62.8 billion in December 2006 to £26.8 billion in late 2010. The evidence from these two cases is rather unclear; it suggests that good risk management can help in avoiding a crisis but it may not be hugely useful in adding value rather than preventing its collapse. More research is needed in this area to test the untested suggestion that risk management is a value adding function.

Summary

In using evidence from the case studies to identify what is needed to join the three dimensions that make up an ERM system, it has been shown that embedding risk management across the entire organization is problematic and requires:

- Clearly stated corporate objectives that are broken down and applied to all levels of the organization.
- Performance targets that are specified at all levels.
- Risk maps that allocate responsibility and are linked to performance targets at an individual level.
- Consistency between rewards for performance and levels of risk acceptable to the organization.
- A risk function that is performance oriented and not compliance focused.

Lessons from the public sector

Successive government policies have promoted the idea that the public sector needs to adopt private sector management techniques in order to improve their efficiency and effectiveness. The case studies of Birmingham City Council and the DCMS demonstrated how their thinking in risk management was influenced by private sector practice in the field. In reflecting on the lessons to be gleaned from comparing the four organizations studied in this book, it seems to be the case that in terms of risk management, the public sector can teach some things to the private sector. The lessons relate to:

- The creation of structures to link strategic objectives to day-to-day operations and
- The development of systems to manage complex risks, e.g. partnership risks and interdependent risks.

The public sector appears more adept in these areas because it has been forced to face complex interrelated risks which cannot be transferred. Even though child protection is a very difficult and expensive service, some aspects of which can be outsourced, a local council remains statutorily responsible for children within its area. Tools to manage the associated risks must therefore be developed.

The first step towards recognizing the interdependence of risks within an organization is risk identification. If it is acknowledged that another department or business unit is affected by a risk, then they need to be informed and given some input into its management. This may take the form of shared responsibilities or simply an oversight role. At the same time, the risk needs also to be escalated to a level where it is monitored by someone who has power over all of the affected parties. So, for example, in a city council, risks which are shared between two services – say education and social services – may be allocated to individuals in each service for the purposes of operational management, but oversight will be at a senior level – the equivalent of board level – within the council. The process is simply one of escalating responsibility for interdependent risks to an appropriate level ensures that the potential impact outside the single service is recognized and monitored. Good communication lies at the heart of such a system.

Internally interdependent risks are not very different from partnership risks, which the public sector also seems to be getting good at managing. One example of how the public sector has developed tools for this purpose relates to the planning and preparation for the 2012 Olympics in London. Whilst sport falls under the remit of the DCMS, operational responsibility for the Olympics lies with the Olympic Delivery Authority (ODA), which was established by Act of Parliament (London Olympic Games and Paralympic Games Act) in 2006. The Act grants specific powers to the ODA which is answerable to government, the Greater London Authority and a range of other stakeholders. By shifting responsibility across to a specially created authority, the risk has been transferred out of the DCMS. Consequently, any problems such as, for example, cost overruns will not impact the department directly, although the reputation risk will still remain with government. The ODA's objective is to make sure the venues and infrastructure for the London 2012 Games are delivered on time, to budget and are fit for purpose. The risks attached to this objective are not only vast in number, but also of a nature that means they potentially impact upon many other parties, both private and public sector e.g. via the disruption to local transport services during the construction of new rail links to the game venues. Additionally, the construction work for the Games is contracted out to the private sector, and so partnership risks are created that need to be managed.

Partnership risk is widespread across the public sector and, as illustrated above, can be found wherever a department opts to share provision of a service with an external party, from either the private or the third sector. Such partnerships create risks for the department because they need to be certain that their objectives are being met, and not impeded by a lack of ability to perform or lack of accountability on the side of the partner. As such, the legal status of the partnership arrangement and the respective areas of responsibility and accountability need to be carefully documented and agreed.

Within Birmingham City Council, the view is taken that such partnerships are essential to the council's strategies but pose key risks and so a senior Board member (Deputy Leader) carries executive responsibility for their oversight. All council partnership arrangements have been mapped and responsibility for their day-to-day monitoring is held immediately below board level. Birmingham Audit has published a partnership risk toolkit, which details the risk management systems applicable to all partnerships (Birmingham, 2007) and argues that:

Stakeholders in the partnership should achieve a common understanding of:

- The potential risks associated with achieving partnership objectives.
- Their relative seriousness.
- How they can be managed.

The systems used for risk management within any partnership are the same as those for the council overall. For example, responsibility for risk management is held by a member of the partnership board and partnership documentation is required to include full details of what systems are in place to monitor, review and evaluate risk and who is responsible for ensuring this is done. This includes the maintenance of joint risk registers which clarify ownership of particular risks. At the same time, risks within the partnership are required to reflect the council's overall appetite for risk. Business continuity plans are therefore also an essential part of the partnership documentation.

In summary, the public sector has developed highly structured approaches to managing and monitoring risks that fall outside the direct control of a single department or council. By drafting clear guidelines such as the Birmingham partnership toolkit, and by extending the application of internal risk management systems into the partnership, any new risks are managed tightly and in a systematic way. For private sector organizations, moving increasingly into network-based ways of working, it is therefore concluded that there are potential lessons to be learnt from the public sector in relation to managing partnership risks, even if the terminology may be slightly different.

Conclusion

It is helpful to summarize this chapter by confirming the key lessons that emerge from analysis of the four case studies:

- Overall objectives and risk appetite need to be clearly specified and communicated across the whole organization.
- Effective risk management need not be bureaucratic in style.
- Compliance alone does not equal effective risk management.
- Risk and performance are best managed in tandem. If staff bonuses are linked to performance measures that are not risk weighted, there is a real danger of encouraging uncontrolled risk taking.
- Effective risk management requires that attention is paid to interdependent risks that cut across business lines.
- Partnership risk(s) can be managed if a carefully structured approach is consistently applied and risks are regularly monitored at a senior level.

Above all, the lesson from this book is that governance regulations and risk management standards are just a starting point. All risk management systems need to be sensitive to context and that means they will be individual to each organization. There remains, however, extensive scope for learning about best practice by sharing ideas and information across organizations.

References

Chenhall, R. H. (2003) 'Management control systems design within its organizational context: findings from contingency-based research and directions for the future', *Accounting, Organizations and Society*, Vol. 28, pp. 127–68.

CIMA (2002) *Risk Management: A Guide to Good Practice*, CIMA, London.

Treasury Committee (2009) *Banking Crisis: Reforming Corporate Governance and Pay in the City*, Ninth Report of Session 2008–9, House of Commons, London.

Woods, M. (2009) 'A contingency theory perspective on the risk management control system within Birmingham City Council', *Management Accounting Research*, Vol. 20, pp. 69–81.

Notes

4 Case study: Tesco PLC

1 *Financial Times*, 19 November 2004.
2 A convenience store is defined as one with a floor area of less than 280 m² which serves a local community and offers extended opening hours that include Sundays.
3 For the 2009 financial year the retention rate equalled 87 per cent. Retention is defined as the percentage of employees who have stayed with the business for longer than one year.
4 The Executive Committee is a subdivision of the Board, chaired by the Chief Executive and comprising all executive directors plus the Company Secretary.
5 The schemes work as follows. *Shares in Success:* shares in the company are allocated to participants in the scheme up to HMRC-approved limits (currently £3,000 per annum). The amount of profit allocated to the scheme is determined by the Board, taking account of company performance. *Buy as you Earn:* an HMRC-approved share purchase scheme under which employees invest up to a limit of £110 on a four-weekly basis to buy shares at the market value in Tesco PLC. *Save as you Earn:* an HMRC-approved savings-related share option scheme under which employees save up to a limit of £250 on a four-weekly basis via a bank or building society with an option to buy shares in Tesco PLC at the end of a three-year or five-year period at a discount of up to 20 per cent of the market value. There are no performance conditions attached to SAYE options.

5 Case study: Royal Bank of Scotland

1 See Patrick Hosking, 'Hubris to nemesis: how Sir Fred Goodwin became the "world's worst banker"', *TimesOnLine* at http://business.timesonline.co.uk/tol/business/economics/article5549510.ece
2 Compliance with the Combined Code forms part of the listing rules of the London Stock Exchange.
3 Criticisms of the FSA's application of the risk based approach fall outside the scope of this case study but make interesting reading for anyone requiring more detail on the regulation of banks in the UK.
4 For further details see, for example, Hull (2007: Chapter 7, pp. 167–94).
5 VaR has, however, come under extensive criticism. See, for example, M. Woods, K. Dowd and C. Humphrey, 'The value of risk reporting: a critical analysis of value-at-risk disclosures in the banking sector', *International Journal of Financial Services Management*, Vol. 8: 1 (2008), pp. 45–64.

6 Case study: The Department of Culture, Media and Sport

1 The Orange Book was reissued in 2004 and extended to include comment upon the lessons learnt about risk management over the intervening period.
2 The original framework is available at http://www.hm-treasury.gov.uk/media//7B1D9/ risk_assessment_framework_220903.pdf. The assessment framework has since been reissued but the basic content remains unchanged. The latest version can be downloaded from http://www.hm-treasury.gov.uk/d/riskmanagement_assessment_framework 220709. pdf
3 The Office of Government Commerce (OGC) is an independent office of HM Treasury, established to help government deliver Best Value from its spending. It provides advice and assistance to central government departments and other public bodies in relation to commercial activities such as procurement, project management and estate management. The OGC has its own pro-forma framework for the management of risks associated with commercial projects.
4 The senior management structure was recently revised, and this description relates to the format as of June 2009.
5 Turnbull included a requirement for private sector companies to prepare annual statements on internal control and to summarize the process used to review the effectiveness of the internal control system. In 2000 the Treasury introduced a requirement for the Accounting Officers of all central government bodies to include a signed Statement on Internal Control (SIC) within their annual accounts from 2001–2 onwards.
6 Further information on PSAs is published on the HM Treasury web site at http://www. hm-treasury.gov.uk/pbr_csr07_psaindex.htm
7 Local Area Agreements (LAAs) are three year agreements, developed by local councils with their partners in a local strategic partnership (LSP). LAAs were first introduced in 2004/5 and, as of June 2008, LAAs are in place for all 150 upper tier local authority areas in England. As defined by the government, a Local Area Agreement 'Sets out the 'deal' between central government and local authorities and their partners to improve the quality of life for local people. As such, the LAA is also a shorter term delivery mechanism for the Sustainable Community Strategy (SCS)' (source: http://www.idea. gov.uk/idk/core/page.do?pageId = 6908743#contents-1).

7 Case study: Birmingham City Council

1 See http://www.audit-commission.gov.uk/localgov/audit/cpa/Pages/Default.aspx for links to information on all of these stages of performance evaluation.
2 The Core Cities Group is a network of England's major regional cities: Birmingham, Bristol, Leeds, Liverpool, Manchester, Newcastle, Nottingham and Sheffield. They form the economic and urban cores of surrounding territories, the city regions.
3 It is important to note that the management structure evolves over time: Figure 7.1 shows the position as at April 2009 but the structure may be expected to change as council services are devolved and localized.
4 The Resources Directorate encompasses Birmingham Audit, Corporate Finance and Asset Management, Corporate Human Resources, Customer Services, Equalities and Diversity, Revenues and Payments, and Service Birmingham (ICT).

Index

ABN AMRO 73, 91, 93, 94
accountability: Birmingham City Council
127; DCMS 111; Good Governance
Standards for Public Services 127;
partnerships 165; public sector 158–9;
Tesco 65, 157, 161
acquisitions: Royal Bank of Scotland
72, 73; Tesco 47–8
ACT *see* Association of Corporate
Treasurers
action plans: Birmingham City Council
142, 143, 144, 145; Modernizing
Government 100; risk register template
35; Tesco 68
AIRMIC *see* Association of Insurance and
Risk Managers
ALARM *see* Association of Local
Authority Risk Managers
AMA *see* Advanced Measurement
Approach
Anderson & Associates 94
ARROW framework 78–9, 158
AS/NZS 4360 standard 13, 27, 28, 32,
33, 130
Association of Corporate Treasurers
(ACT) 39
Association of Insurance and Risk
Managers (AIRMIC) 37, 130
Association of Local Authority Risk
Managers (ALARM) 37, 103, 130
assurance statements 125, 135
AstraZeneca 101
Audit Commission 128, 129, 130, 146, 147
Audit Committees 38, 39–40; Birmingham
City Council 129; DCMS 111, 119, 122;
Royal Bank of Scotland 84, 85, 90, 91;
Tesco 61, 63, 64
auditing 10, 37, 156; Birmingham City
Council 134, 135–6, 143, 146, 152;

DCMS 109, 121–2; IRM risk
management process 67, 113; Lehman
Brothers 17; risk architecture 38; Royal
Bank of Scotland 81–2, 90; Tesco 61,
63–5, 68
Australia 13, 27, 28, 76, 130

balanced scorecard 58, 161; (see also
Tesco steering wheel 57–60; 167)
Bank of China 72
banking crisis (2007/8) 2, 14, 15–16,
19–20, 73
Barclays Bank 24
Basel Accords 77–8, 79–80, 87–8, 158
BCCI 10
benchmarking 101, 102, 103, 124
Best Practice 19; examples 101, 127; in
governance codes 76; public sector 99,
105, 127; Royak Bank of Scotland 91;
sharing 103
Best Value 128, 152, 170n3
Birmingham City Council 2, 127–52,
156, 157, 158–9; city profile 130–1;
council profile 131; governance model
131–3; internal audit 135–6, 143, 152;
key statistics 132; motivation to adopt
risk management 133–4; partnerships
165–6; performance management 130,
135, 146–51, 160, 161; portfolio-based
risk management 163; risk management
framework 137–46; risk management
strategy 134; risk maps 161; senior
management 134–5
Blair, Tony 99
Boards of Directors 39, 42; annual review
135; codes of governance 9, 10, 11, 77;
DCMS 108, 111; risk architecture 38;
Royal Bank of Scotland 82, 84; Sarbanes
Oxley Act 76; Tesco 55, 61–3, 64, 65

Bostock, Nathan 93
BP 23, 101
Buffett, Warren 23–4

Cadbury Report (1992) 100, 125, 135
Canada 12, 13, 28, 76
capital adequacy ratios 77–8, 88, 158
capital risk 90
Central Government Special Interest
    Group (IRM) 103
change 26, 114
Change4Life campaign 104
Chartered Institute of Management
    Accountants (CIMA) 29, 51, 93,
    136, 159
Chartered Institute of Public Finance and
    Accountancy (CIPFA) 127, 129, 134,
    135, 136
Chief Risk Officer (CRO) 2, 40–1, 90,
    91–2, 93, 95- 96
Churchill 72
CIMA *see* Chartered Institute of
    Management Accountants
CIPFA *see* Chartered Institute of Public
    Finance and Accountancy
Citibank 14
Citizens' Bank 72
Coca-Cola 24
CoCO (*Criteria of Control Board
    Guidance on Control*) 12, 13, 15, 28
codes of governance 1–2, 9, 10–11,
    18–20, 76–7, 134; 'comply or explain'
    approach 19; COSO 2002 framework
    12–13; COSO 2004 framework 15, 27,
    28–33, 130; COSO cube 30.
Cohen, Jack 47
Combined Code (UK) 12, 18, 41, 76, 77,
    158, 169n2
Committee of Sponsoring Organizations
    (COSO) 10–12, 19, 76, 160; ERM
    framework 15, 27, 28–31, 32, 33, 130;
    Lehman Brothers annual report 17
communication of risks 2, 37;
    Birmingham City Council 136;
    DCMS 165; Royal Bank of Scotland
    162; Tesco 68, 69
'comply or explain' codes 18, 19, 20
Comprehensive Performance Assessment
    (CPA) 128–9, 134, 139–40, 146; key
    lines of enquiry (KLOE) for
    risk assessment 129
consultation 37
contingency planning 116

contingency theory 159
control environment 12, 30; *see also*
    internal control
corporate governance 9–21; banking crisis
    15–16, 19–20; Birmingham City
    Council 134; 'hard' versus 'soft' laws
    18–19; multi layered 18; regulatory
    change 10–16, 76–7; risk management
    and 9–10; Royal Bank of Scotland 84;
    Tesco 55–60, 61, 157; *see also*
    governance
Corporate Governance Code (UK) 1–2,
    9–20
corporate treasurers 40
COSO *see* Committee of Sponsoring
    Organizations
costs of control 143
country risk 23, 25
CPA *see* Comprehensive Performance
    Assessment
credit risk 23, 25; Basel II 80; quantifica-
    tion of 94–5; Royal Bank of Scotland
    84, 86, 88, 90, 91, 93, 95; Credit Suisse
    First Boston 14
crime 23, 86–7
CRO *see* Chief Risk Officer
customers: as priority 159; Royal Bank
    of Scotland 82; Tesco 52, 53, 57, 58,
    156–7

data protection 24, 103
DCMS *see* Department for Culture, Media
    and Sport
De Haas, M. 68
Den Braber, Ron 95
Department for Culture, Media and Sport
    (DCMS) 2, 99, 106–26, 156, 157,
    158–9, 165; Change4Life campaign
    104; governance structure 108–10;
    guidance 105; internal audit 121–2;
    Internal Audit Services (IAS) 111;
    key statistics 107; monitoring 118–21;
    overview 106–8; partnership risk 124–5;
    performance management 123–4,
    161–2; risk assessment 115–18; risk
    identification 112–15; risk management
    framework 112, 113; self-assessment
    122–4
derivatives 80, 81, 89, 95
disclosure 37, 38, 79–80
Disclosures Committee 38
domain-specific risk management
    103–6

economic risk 114
Economist Intelligence Unit (EIU) 23
embedding of risk management 42, 156,
    159, 160, 163–4; Audit Commission
    inspections 129; Birmingham City
    Council 135, 136, 137; DCMS 112, 118;
    Enterprise Risk Management 41; gov-
    ernment departments 102; ISO 31000
    standard 28, 32; performance plans 151;
    risk architecture 38; Tesco 55; Turnbull
    Report 13
employees: Birmingham City Council
    136; linked to customers 159; Tesco 52,
    59–60, 66, 70, 169n3
Enron 1, 13–14, 18, 76
Enterprise Risk Management (ERM) 2,
    5–6, 155; COSO framework 15, 27,
    28–31, 32, 33, 130, 160; definition of
    29; embedding of risk management 41;
    implementation 163; organizational
    culture 33; in practice 38–9; risk mea-
    surement problems 75; Royal Bank of
    Scotland 90, 91; standardization 22
Entertainment UK (EUK) 25
environmental risk 26, 114
ERF *see* Executive Risk Forum
ERM *see* Enterprise Risk Management
EUK *see* Entertainment UK
European Corporate Governance Forum
    18–19, 21
events logs 145
Executive Risk Forum (ERF) 84, 85, 92

feedback 37, 118, 143, 151, 156
financial crisis (2007/8) 2, 14, 15–16,
    19–20, 39, 73
financial economists 40
financial instruments 80, 89, 95, 158
financial risk 23, 25; DCMS 124; Tesco
    54–5; Value at Risk 80
Financial Services Authority (FSA) 78–9,
    82, 88
foreign exchange risk 23, 25, 36–7, 40
fraud 86–7, 89; Audit Commission
    inspections 129; Birmingham City
    Council 146; financial reporting 10–12;
    IT risk 24
FSA *see* Financial Services Authority
funding risk 88, 90

GAC *see* Group Audit Committee
GALCO *see* Group Asset and Liability
    Management Committee

GARP *see* Global Association of Risk
    Professionals
GCC *see* Group Credit Committee
GCEAG *see* Group Chief Executive's
    Advisory Group
GE Capital 41
Gelband, Michael 95
generic risk management 103–6
Global Association of Risk Professionals
    (GARP) 93
Global Crossing 14, 18
Goldman Sachs 14
Good Governance Standards for Public
    Services 127
Goodwin, Sir Fred 75
Gossage, Richard 93
governance 9–21; banking crisis 15–16,
    19–20; Birmingham City Council
    131–3, 134; CIPFA framework 127;
    DCMS 108–10, 114; 'hard' versus 'soft'
    laws 18–19; multi layered 18; regulatory
    change 10–16, 76–7; risk management
    and 9–10; Royal Bank of Scotland 84;
    Tesco 55–60, 61, 157; *see also* codes of
    governance
Government Olympic Executive 108
Green Book (HM Treasury, 1997) 100
Greenspan, Alan 18
guidance, public sector 103–6
Gupta, P. 13

Helliar, C. V. 64
HM Treasury 99, 100, 101, 105, 109, 122,
    170n5
Hood, C. 103
horizon scanning 89–90, 114
HSBC 24
human capital 23, 24
Hutter, B. 41
Hydro One 41
identification of risk *see* risk
    identification
IFAC *see* International Federation of
    Accountants
impact of risk 34, 36; Audit
    Commission inspections 129;
    Birmingham City Council 140–1,
    142; DCMS 115–17
implementation 32–3, 136, 163
information technology (IT) 23, 24–5;
    Birmingham City Council 144–6;
    Tesco 62–3
Institute of Internal Audit 136

Institute of Risk Management (IRM):
Central Government Special Interest
Group 103; examinations 136; risk
management process 60, 66–7, 112,
113; risk management standards 28,
37, 130
interdependent risks 2, 75, 115, 157, 159,
163, 164–5, 166
internal control 9, 10; banking crisis
15–16; Birmingham City Council 135;
Combined Code 77; Comprehensive
Performance Assessment 128–9; COSO
framework 12–13, 19, 28, 29–31, 160;
DCMS 109, 111–12, 124; government
departments 102, 106; internal audits
37; Lehman Brothers 16, 17; narrow
versus broad definitions of 16;
Sarbanes Oxley Act 14–15, 19;
Tesco 63, 70; *see also* risk control
internal environment 12, 30
International Federation of Accountants
(IFAC) 29
IRM *see* Institute of Risk Management
ISO 31000 standard 27–8, 31–8
ISO Guide 22

J. P. Morgan 14, 80

Kelly, Kate 95
key performance indicators (KPIs) 52, 58,
59, 157
King Code of Corporate Governance for
South Africa (2009) 10, 16
Kleingeld, A. 68
KLOE *see* key lines of enquiry
K-One Technology 36–7
KPIs *see* key performance indicators
KPMG 90

LAAs *see* Local Area Agreements
Lam, James 41
leadership 10, 101, 122, 123
Leahy, Sir Terence 47, 49, 52–3, 54, 69
legal risk 114
Lehman Brothers 16, 17, 95
likelihood consequences assessment 34,
36; Arrow Framework 78–79;
Birmingham City Council 140–1,
142; DCMS 115–17; ISO31000 33–34;
Tesco 66–67
liquidity risk 86, 88, 90
Local Area Agreements (LAAs) 121, 148,
170n7

Local Government Association 127
Long Term Capital Management 76

Magique software 145–6
market discipline 78, 79–80
market risk 23, 25; Basel II 80; Royal
Bank of Scotland 84, 86, 88, 90, 91, 93;
silo-based management 94; Value at
Risk models 83, 95
Markets in Financial Instruments80, 89
Marks and Spencer 26
Martin, William 93
Maxwell Group 10
McKillop, Sir Tom 73, 75
McNamee, D. 64
minimum capital requirements 78, 79;
see also capital adequacy ratios
Modernizing Government Action Plan 100
monitoring: Birmingham City Council
136, 143, 151; COSO framework 12,
30, 31; DCMS 118–21; government
departments 102; integration of risk and
performance management 162; IRM
risk management process 67, 113; ISO
31000 standard 33, 37; oversight teams
156; partnerships 166; Tesco 61, 66, 68
multi agency working 104

NAO *see* National Audit Office
Nathaniel, Peter 93
National Audit Office (NAO) 100, 101,
102, 106, 109
National Portrait Gallery 122
natural hazards 23, 25
NatWest 72, 73
Netherlands 11, 13, 18
New Public Management 40, 99–100, 158
New York Stock Exchange 76
New Zealand 13, 27, 28
Nike 24, 25

OECD Principles of Corporate
Governance 11
Office of Government Commerce (OGC)
105, 124, 170n3
Ohmae, Kenichi 52
Olympic and Paralympic Games (2012)
108, 109, 119, 165
One Stop 48
operational risk 26; Basel II 80; DCMS
114, 120, 124; quantification of 95;
Royal Bank of Scotland 82, 84, 86, 88,
90, 91, 93; silo-based management 94

Orange Book (HM Treasury, 2000) 101, 105, 112, 170n1
organizational culture: embedding of risk management 156; in governance codes 9, 20, 30; risk awareness 1–2, 32, 33;

Page, M. 9–10
partnerships: Birmingham City Council 2, 165–6; DCMS 114, 118, 121, 124–5; government Risk Improvement programme 101; London 2012 Olympic Games 165
Partnerships and Programmes Directorate (DCMS) 108
Pearson, Karl 95
Peecher, M. 14
performance management 51, 160–2, 164, 166; Birmingham City Council 130, 135, 146–51, 160, 161; Comprehensive Performance Assessment 128–9, 134, 139–40, 146; DCMS 123–4, 161–2; government departments 102; Tesco 52, 53, 59, 60–6, 71, 157–8, 160, 161
Peters, Tom 22
Peter's Committee Report (1997) 13
planning 147, 148, 151, 160
political risk 23, 25; Birmingham City Council 147; DCMS 114; public sector 158; Royal Bank of Scotland 88
Polly Peck 10
portfolio-based risk management 159, 163
Power, Michael 19–20, 41
price risk 66
professionalization of risk 2, 10, 40, 93, 103, 136
profit sharing 60, 70, 169n5
Public Company Accounting Oversight Board 17
public sector 2, 5, 158–9; Audit Committees 39–40; Comprehensive Performance Assessment 128–9; CRO role 41; generic versus domain-specific approaches 103–6; historical background 99–103; lessons from the 129, 164–5, 166; *see also* Birmingham City Council; Department for Culture, Media and Sport
Public Sector Benchmarking Service (PSBS) 103, 105
Public Service Agreements (PSAs) 119

Quantitative based risk management 39, 49, 80, 82–83, 86, 90, 94–5

RAG (red, amber, green) assessment 34–6, 67, 83, 117, 120, 140
RBS *see* Royal Bank of Scotland
Rebonato, Ricardo 95
regulation: banking 24, 77–80, 81; corporate governance 10–16, 18–19, 76–7; Royal Bank of Scotland 87–8, 89–90, 158; Tesco 62, 63; *see also* standards
regulatory risk 23, 24; Royal Bank of Scotland 87, 91; Tesco 62, 63
remuneration 60, 64
reputation risk 23–4, 26, 29; Birmingham City Council 147; DCMS 118, 124, 125; Royal Bank of Scotland 87
residual risk 34, 35, 67; Birmingham City Council 143, 144, 145; DCMS 117; IRM risk management process 67, 113; Royal Bank of Scotland 82
responsibility for risk management 39–41, 42, 161, 164; Birmingham City Council 134–7, 138; DCMS 115, 116, 118, 119, 121; interdependent risks 164–5; partnerships 165, 166; performance plans 151; public sector 104, 128; Royal Bank of Scotland 91; Tesco 61–6; *see also* risk ownership
review: Birmingham City Council 136, 143; government departments 102; ISO 31000 standard 37; supervisory review for banks 78, 79; Tesco 63
risk, definitions of 22, 109–12, 134
risk appetite 33, 34, 166; Birmingham City Council 142–3, 166; Boards of Directors 39, 42; changes in 36; COSO framework 29, 30; DCMS116–7 private sector 159; Royal Bank of Scotland 82–3; Tesco 61–2, 64
risk architecture 2, 37–8, 40, 42
risk assessment and evaluation 34–36; ARROW framework 78–9; Birmingham City Council 140–142; COSO framework, 28, 30, 31; DCMS 115–18; government departments 100–1; IRM risk management process, 67, 113; ISO 31000 standard 33–4; Royal Bank of Scotland 89, 90; Tesco 60–61, 67
risk categories 22–7; banking 81; Birmingham City Council 139–40; DCMS 114, 115; Royal Bank of Scotland 84–9; Tesco 62, 67

risk control 36, 134; accountants 40;
  Birmingham City Council 143; DCMS
  120; Enterprise Risk Management 38;
  prioritization of risks 142; Royal Bank
  of Scotland 81; Tesco 61–2; *see also*
  internal control
risk disclosures and reporting 37, 38,
  79–80, 169n5; Birmingham City
  Council 138, 151; central government
  guidance 105; DCMS 113, 122; Royal
  Bank of Scotland 80, 90–92; \tesco
  60–61, 67–68
risk identification: Birmingham City
  Council 136, 137, 139–40, 144; COSO
  framework 29, 30, 31; DCMS 112–15;
  interdependent risks 164; ISO 31000
  standard 33–4; Tesco 61, 62–3
Risk Improvement programme (UK, 2004)
  101, 103, 158
Risk and performance management
  160, 161;
Risk Leadership Forum 92–3
risk management, definition of 93
risk management ,framework: Birmingham
  City Council 137–46; DCMS 112, 113;
  ISO 31, 32–3; Royal Bank of Scotland
  83–93; Tesco 66–8
risk management, objectives
  Birmingham City Council 134; CIMA
  29; Comprehensive Performance
  Assessment 129; COSO 28–9; DCMS
  112–3; principles 156; Royal Bank of
  Scotland 83; Tesco 60
risk management of cross cutting or
  interdependent risks 139, 146, 164–166
risk management principles 31, 32
risk management process: Birmingham
  City Council 142–3; IRM 67, 112, 113;
  ISO 31, 33–7
risk managers, power of 95–96
risk maps 64, 161
risk ownership: Audit Commission
  inspections 129; Birmingham City
  Council 143, 161; DCMS 115, 118, 120;
  Royal Bank of Scotland 91; Tesco 68;
  see also responsibility for risk
  management
risk registers 34, 35; Birmingham City
  Council 139, 143, 144; DCMS 119, 120,
  121; partnerships 166; Tesco 62, 68
risk self assessment 122–124; Risk Support Team (HM Treasury) 99, 101
risk transfer 36, 134
risk treatment 36–7, 67, 113

Rothstein, H. 103
Royal Bank of Scotland (RBS) 2, 72–96,
  156, 157; company history 72–3; core
  divisions and brands 73–4; FSA
  assessment 78; governance structure 84;
  Group Asset and Liability Management
  Committee (GALCO) 84, 85, 92; Group
  Audit Committee (GAC) 84, 85; Group
  Chief Executive's Advisory Group
  (GCEAG) 84, 85; Group Credit
  Committee (GCC) 84, 85; Group
  Executive Management Committee
  (GEMC) 84, 85, 91; Group Risk
  Committee (GRC) 84, 85, 92; group
  risk management (GRM) 81, 83, 84, 93;
  Group Risk Management Committee
  (GRMC) 38; horizon scanning 89–90;
  insurance 72, 74, 86, 88, 90; key
  observations 75; key statistics 74;
  managerial power 95–6; market
  capitalization 163; performance
  management 162; 'quants' 94–5;
  reporting lines 91–2; responsibility for
  risk management 91; risk appetite 82–3;
  risk categories 84–9; risk management
  function 81–2, 158; risk management
  objectives 83; silo-based management
  94, 158; stock market listings 73;
  support structures 92–3; Tesco Personal
  Finance 48, 55, 68, 70

Sarbanes Oxley Act (SOX, 2002) 14–16,
  18, 19, 21, 29, 76, 89–90, 158
scandals 10, 13–14, 76
Securities and Exchange Commission
  (SEC) 14–15, 76
security risks 23, 114
Selim, G. 64

SIC *see* Statement on Internal Control
silo-based management 13, 70, 94, 158,
  159, 162, 163
Society of Local Authority Chief
  Executives (SOLACE) 127, 134
SOLACE *see* Society of Local Authority
  Chief Executives
Solomon, I. 14
South Africa 10
SOX *see* Sarbanes Oxley Act
Spira, L. 9–10
standards 1, 13, 16, 27–38, 41; AS/NZS
  4360 standard 13, 27, 28, 32, 33, 130;
  COSO framework 28–31; Good
  Governance Standards for Public

Services 127; ISO 31000 standard 27–8, 31–8; local authorities 130; Public Company Accounting Oversight Board 17; risk categories 26; *see also* regulation
Statement on Internal Control (SIC) 102, 105, 109, 111–12, 122, 124, 135, 170n5
steering wheel (Tesco) 57–60, 66, 157
strategic risk: DCMS 119–21, 122, 123; reactive management of 159
strategy 26, 28, 156; Birmingham City Council 134; COSO framework 29; government Risk Improvement programme 101; Ohmae on 52; strategic fit 51; Tesco 55, 57, 61, 156–7
supply chain risk 25, 54, 62
systemic risk 104

T & S Stores 48
targets: Birmingham City Council 147–51; cascaded through organization 160, 161; Comprehensive Performance Assessment 139–40; DCMS 114; embedding of risk management 164; Tesco 57–8, 60, 66, 70; *see also* objectives; performance management
technological risk 114; *see also* information technology
terrorism 23, 25
Tesco 2, 41, 47–71, 156–8, 159; company history 47–8, 49; competitors 48; corporate culture 53; geographic spread of operations 49; governance 55–60; influence of Leahy 52–3; key statistics 50; nature of the business 53–4; organizational structure 54–5; overseas site acquisition 64, 65; performance management 52, 53, 59, 60–6, 157–8, 160, 161; portfolio-based risk management 163; reporting and communication 68, 69; risk management framework 66–8; steering wheel 57–60, 66, 157; stock market listings 48; store formats 48
Tesco Express 48
Tesco Metro 47, 48
Tesco Personal Finance 48, 49, 55, 68–70
Tett, Gillian 80
'Three lines of defence' model 81, 82
training 93, 136, 137, 145
transparency: banking regulation 79, 80; Good Governance Standards for Public Services 127; ISO 31000 standard 32; public sector 104, 106
Treadway Commission 10–12
Treasury 99, 100, 101, 105, 109, 122, 170n5
Turnbull Report (1999) 12–13, 15, 76–7, 100, 109, 129, 170n5
Tyco 18

Ulster Bank 74
United Kingdom (UK): Combined Code 12, 18, 41, 76, 77, 158, 169n2; 'comply or explain' principle 18; corporate scandals 10; multi layered governance 18; Risk Management Standard 27; Turnbull Report 12–13, 15, 76–7, 100, 109, 129, 170n5
United States (US) 10–12, 13, 18, 73
'upstream risks' 89

Value at Risk (VaR) 80, 83, 95, 169n5
Virgin Megastores 25

Woolworth 25
WorldCom 14, 18, 76

Zavvi 25
Zurich 101